BETTER
IDEAS FOR
CHILDREN'S
WORKERS

100

BETTER IDEAS FOR CHILDREN'S WORKERS

BETTY B. ROBERTSON

BAKER BOOK HOUSE
Grand Rapids, Michigan

Formerly published under the title
A Galaxy of Ideas for Children's Workers

Copyright 1973 by
Beacon Hill Press
Reprinted 1974 by
Baker Book House

ISBN: 0-8010-7621-8

PHOTOLITHOPRINTED BY CUSHING - MALLOY, INC.
ANN ARBOR, MICHIGAN, UNITED STATES OF AMERICA
1974

To my loving husband and
constant companion,
EARL,
this book is
affectionately dedicated.

Contents

Foreword

Let me introduce you to a book that deals with two basic problems faced by workers with children: (1) how to find new ideas, and (2) how to put those ideas to work in a local situation. This book does not come to you as a complete solution to these problems, but it does come with a "galaxy of ideas" that are starters. Betty Robertson has drawn her ideas from her personal experiences in her work with boys and girls. As you read this book, form a mental picture of your group and their particular needs; then let these ideas filter through. Much as in any exploration, the unexpected will be found. An idea may lead you to another idea, and that eventually to a more effective ministry to boys and girls. This is not a cut-and-dried, do-it-like-it-is-printed type of book, but more like putting a car in gear.

So I recommend this book to you for a journey through a "galaxy of ideas" to a soft landing right where your needs are. And remember this, we didn't find out everything on the first trip to the moon, so keep this book handy and explore it often.

—BILL YOUNG

General Director, Camps, Caravan, and Junior Fellowship Church of the Nazarene

INTRODUCTION:

THE CHALLENGE OF CHILDREN

How often do we really stop to recognize the potential of our children? Every child who comes into the world presents a new possibility for lifting the destiny of the human race. God has made response a natural thing in the life of a child. But the nature of that response—the direction it takes—is determined in a large measure by the influence of those adults who are important in that child's everyday life. As Christian adult leaders we must accept our responsibility with children by doing everything within our power to lead them in the paths of righteousness.

God's interest in the nurturing of a child's responsiveness to Him is just as great today as it was the day Jesus set a child in the center of the disciples and said, "Whosoever receives one of such children in My name receives Me." When we accept the responsibility of helping children in their spiritual growth, we also help ourselves to grow spiritually. Do you really want to know what it means to receive Christ in all His fullness? Then accept the challenge of children!

The child is the pivot around which all other elements of a children's program turn. He is the reason for everything else which is involved. And since every member of the class is different in some ways from every other member, knowing the pupil must be the beginning point of planning. His needs guide us in setting up objectives.

One of the child's basic needs is to be loved. He needs to be told and shown that he is loved. A pupil must have the assurance that he belongs, and that if he is absent, he is missed. Children need also to feel that they are achieving —accomplishing tasks appropriate to their abilities. It is natural for boys and girls to want to learn. As teachers, we should consider their questions seriously. Another very important need that children have is to feel needed and important. They desire attention and approval from both adults and their peers. Favorable recognition should be given for a job well done—and variety of activities should be provided, so all children can succeed at something.

Children are not miniature adults. They are persons going through the normal stages of development, as God planned. They need teachers who are able to understand the child's present stage of development and how to guide him. These general characteristics may be learned through reading and observation.

The objectives for developing an effective children's ministry should include:

1. Leading each child in a personal relationship with Christ.

2. Laying a solid foundation and beginning the development of character that is Christlike.

3. Helping the child develop a Christian philosophy of life on his own level of growth and maturity.

4. Helping boys and girls develop the ability to meet all the experiences of life with adequate spiritual resources.

There are many ideas and methods which can be used in launching and developing a children's ministry in the local church. This book contains some which have been used successfully. Perhaps they will help you as you accept the challenge of working with children.

1. SUNDAY SCHOOL

SPECIAL DAYS

Special days in the Sunday school are planned to encourage boys and girls to be regular in attendance. These Sundays also provide opportunity for the children to invite their friends to attend with them. Care should always be taken that this kind of promotion does not use time intended for the teaching-learning process.

You Have the Key!

This theme may be used in several different ways.

1. Mail a paper key to each pupil during the week. Include a note stating that if the key is brought to Sunday school the next week it will open the Treasure Chest and the child will receive a free gift.

2. Fasten paper keys under various chairs in the department. Boys and girls sitting in the marked chairs take their keys to the Treasure Chest and receive a free gift.

3. Provide a box of real keys, only a few of which fit the chest. Each child selects a key and tries to open the chest. If his key fits, the child receives a free gift.

4. Mail a paper key to each child on the Sunday school and prospect list. Attach a note stating that the "key" to opening the Treasure Chest is to be present in Sunday school the next week. Everyone in attendance selects a small gift.

Treasure Chest Sundays

Equipment: An old chest decorated to look like a treasure chest.

Incentive: A free gift from the Treasure Chest is given

to everyone who is present in Sunday school on the first Sunday. For the remaining three weeks, a free gift is given to any pupil who brings a friend. Each student in any class with perfect attendance or the equivalent of enrollment in attendance for the month also receives a gift.

Advertisement:

1. On the Sunday prior to the special emphasis, take the Treasure Chest to all departments in the children's division. Build interest by telling the boys and girls how they can unlock the chest and receive a free gift.

2. Mail colorful flyers during the week to acquaint parents with the special emphasis.

3. Run special features in the church newsletter during the month.

4. Use attractive posters in department rooms and classrooms.

B-O-O-M (Bring One Or More) Day

Emphasis: Challenge each student in the entire children's division to bring one or more with him on a designated Sunday.

Features: Have a combined school opening or closing with a well-planned program. Plan top-quality features such as a chalk artist, a ventriloquist, a puppet show, a musical group, or an outstanding children's speaker. Give special recognition to classes with the best percentage of enrollment present.

Incentives: Publicize the number of children wanted that Sunday in the children's division. Have a reserved section for all children's classes in the opening or closing program. Emphasize that this is a great opportunity to "bring one or more" friends. A small prize may be given to each one who brings one or more; or a Polaroid picture might be taken of those who bring someone with them that day.

12

Three Special Surprise Sundays

Incentive: A small gift is given to everyone who brings a friend during the three "Special Surprise Sundays." The top "three" pupils who bring the most over "three" during the "three" Special Surprise Sundays may choose from "three" special gifts.

Advertisement: On the Sunday before launching this emphasis, saturate the church with publicity. Make large posters for bulletin boards; prepare tags for teachers to wear; provide badges for the pupils to pin on as a reminder. During the campaign, mail flyers to the homes, put announcements in the weekly church newsletter, and have the teachers make phone calls to remind students of the special emphasis.

Sundae Sunday

This special day will excite the regular members, interest chronic absentees, and serve as an easy invitation to non-church children. Here are the simple steps:

1. Have posters in each classroom advertising "Sundae Sunday."

2. Make announcements to the pupils and encourage them to bring their friends!

3. Send a letter to each Sunday school pupil and prospect. An attractive letter can be made by tracing a sundae from a pattern or coloring book. The wording could read: "Look what's happening in the children's division! Delicious sundaes will be served to all who attend Sunday school! Bring a friend with you! Don't miss this special day! Special recognition to those who bring friends!"

4. Sundaes can be served either at a central place or taken to each class and served there. Confusion can be eliminated by making the sundaes during the week and freezing them.

Sack Sunday

Mail a small, brown paper sack to older Sunday school children. Insert in the sack a strip of paper on which is written: "Get out of the sack this Sunday morning for a special feature during Sunday school. If you come and bring a friend, our goal will be in the bag! Bring this empty sack Sunday and we will fill it!" Use candy or some other treat or prize to fill the sack.

"Balloon Burst" Day

Select several suitable prizes and write the name of each prize on a slip of paper. Fold each slip and put it inside a balloon. Blow up the balloon and tie a string on the end. Fasten the balloons to a long string stretched across the room.

Whoever is the winner of the particular emphasis gets to break any balloon he chooses, receiving the prize listed inside. Prizes may be given for attendance, bringing visitors, bringing an offering, or anything else that needs special attention.

Bring Your Parents Sunday

Encourage all Sunday school pupils to bring their parents with them. Be sure to provide ushers and greeters to welcome new people and direct everyone to the proper class.

"Kites for Kids" Day

Designate a special Sunday when a free kite will be given to every child present in Sunday school. On the Sunday before "Kite Day," Sunday school workers should wear a small kite giving information about the special day. Send flyers into all homes during the week and run advertisement in the local newspaper.

Mystery Box

A mystery box will boost attendance and create excitement among the boys and girls. Send an advertisement to all children which says: "I will be carrying a box all day. If you attend Sunday school and come up to me anytime on Sunday, and say these exact words, 'I attended Sunday school this morning,' I will give you something from the Mystery Box." The pastor, Sunday school superintendent, or some other person may be responsible for carrying the box.

Five Most Wanted

Make "Wanted" posters to hang in each department. Crazy pictures and fictitious information are placed on each poster to cover up the real purpose. The supervisor selects five prime prospects from the list of absentees. Only the supervisor and teachers know who the "Most Wanted" are. When one of the five comes to Sunday school, a poster is removed. The object is that all the absentees must come in order to get the secret five. If the children are successful in locating the five most wanted, they may be rewarded with a party or some other treat.

Giant Puppet Show

Engage someone in your church or community who is skilled in the use of puppets to plan several special features and at least one exciting story. Construct a puppet stage and backdrop for the event (and store them for future use).

For an attendance incentive, announce that all boys and girls who attend Sunday school for five Sundays in a row will receive a free gift after the puppet show. Also, all children who bring five friends with them to Sunday school will receive a prize.

Use attractive publicity to advertise the giant puppet show. Mail announcements to all members and prospects.

Door-to-door canvassing is also very effective for promoting this type of attendance emphasis.

Operation T.A.D.
(Teacher Appreciation Day)

"Teacher Appreciation Day" lets the boys and girls in the Sunday school show appreciation to their teachers. "Top secret" is the label placed on Operation T.A.D. Send each child a letter the week before this special day, giving these instructions:

"Assignment No. 1: Tie this string on your finger, so you don't forget that this Sunday is 'Teacher Appreciation Day' in the children's division of our Sunday school. [Tape a piece of string to the letter.]

"Assignment No. 2: Seal your lips! The Sunday school teachers don't know anything about this special day. So—shhhhh! Let's surprise them! Don't let the secret out!

"Assignment No. 3: Write a poem—or a letter—or get a little gift to show your appreciation for your teacher. Bring it Sunday, hand it to your teacher, and say, 'Today is "Teacher Appreciation Day." Here's something for you!'"

Children enjoy an opportunity to do something special for their teachers—and the teachers will appreciate this thoughtful gesture.

Secret: Special Delivery

If "Operation T.A.D." is used in the local church one year, try "Secret: Special Delivery" another year. During the week contact each pupil and ask him to write a letter of appreciation for his teacher. Pupils are to bring their letters to church the following Sunday for special delivery "in person." Such an emphasis has the following results:

1. Increased attendance, for each child must be present to bring the letter "in person."

2. Opportunity for creativity as the child writes his expression of appreciation.

3. Encouragement to teachers.

Carrousel of Progress

FIRST SUNDAY—"Getting to Know You"

Find Your Number. Divide the group into pairs and assign each pair a number. Give each child in a pair the name and phone number of his "twin." If both children with the same number are present on Sunday, both mates receive a prize. Each "twin" is to contact the other during the week.

SECOND SUNDAY—"Climb Every Mountain"

Talking Treasure Chest. A hidden tape recorder makes the chest talk. On the Sunday previously, the talking chest visits each department, promising the children that they will receive a prize from the chest for each friend they bring the next Sunday. Each new friend also gets a prize from the chest. Promote the idea by setting a goal and challenging to climb the mountain toward it.

THIRD SUNDAY—"A Place for Us"

A Secret Place. Everyone who brings a friend on this Sunday gets to bring that friend and go to a secret place for a party on the following Saturday. A small prize may also be given to all who are present in Sunday school on this day.

FOURTH SUNDAY—"The Impossible Dream" (our dream is to "Talk to the Animals")

A Trip to the Animal Farm or Zoo. On this Sunday a "talking animal" (a puppet or someone costumed as an animal) visits the Sunday school classes. All new friends, and the children who brought them, receive a gift. PLUS . . . the five children who bring the most new people on this Sunday get to visit an animal farm or zoo the next Saturday.

FIFTH SUNDAY—"O Happy Day"

To McDonald's for a Happy Cup. All children who

bring a new friend get to bring their friends to the church on the following Saturday for a bus ride to a McDonald's hamburger place. Children buy their own food and the church provides the Happy Cups.

During the "Carrousel of Progress" emphasis, each class or department is responsible for:

1. Contest posters for each Sunday.

2. Posting the names of all children who win prizes each week.

3. Securing prizes from the office.

4. Building enthusiasm.

5. Contacting all members weekly.

6. Keeping accurate records of new friends who are enrolled in the department.

Money Store

Print play money in denominations of $1.00, $5.00, $10.00, and $20.00. In the center of each piece write: "This is valuable to you! Don't lose it because it cannot be replaced. You may spend this during the month of June. Bring your friends!" The children receive, for instance, $1.00 for being on time; $5.00 for participation and cooperation; $20.00 for bringing a friend; and so on. A "store" is set up with various items containing price tags and children can "shop" for items.

Operation: Offering Increase

To meet its financial needs, the Sunday school often must find a way to enlarge the weekly offerings. The children's division can put into effect "Operation: Offering Increase."

Designate the first Sunday as "Penny per Pound" Sunday. All pupils and teachers weigh themselves during the week and bring in their Sunday school offering accordingly! Usually the offering will more than double. (No one has to tell how much he is giving.)

Advertise the second Sunday as "Nickel Sunday." Present the challenge to see how many pictures of Thomas Jefferson can be brought to Sunday school. Each department or class devises creative ways of promoting the emphasis within the group.

The final Sunday of "Operation: Offering Increase" is "Dime Sunday." Ask each child to bring "one thin dime" with him. Boys may compete against the girls to see who has the biggest offering for the day.

Flying High

"Keep Our Attendance Flying High" is a good theme for spring. Use kites cut from various colors of construction paper to make an attractive bulletin board. Each Sunday post the class attendance on the kite.

Picture Day

Nothing thrills new parents more than people showing real interest in their babies. Capitalize on this by taking a Polaroid picture of each new baby in the nursery. Give the picture to the parents in an envelope, with a note which reads: "It was a pleasure to have your baby in our Nursery Department. Do hurry back to worship with us again soon. We provide nursery facilities for infants and children up to three years of age during all our services. We invite you to leave your children with us."

CONTESTS

Whenever contests are used, write the rules down so that parents, as well as children, understand. When presenting the contest, discuss with younger children the fact that not all will receive a reward, even though all work hard. Do not let contest promotion interfere with the time needed for the class session.

19

B.O.T.S.S. (Bring Others To Sunday School)

Participants: Grades 1-6

Length of Contest Emphasis: Four weeks

Initial Publicity Push:

1. Mail to each Sunday school teacher an information sheet containing the purpose of the contest, the incentives, prize information, and suggestions for promoting the contest in the class.

2. Each Sunday school worker wears a B.O.T.S.S. button on the Sunday the contest is announced. Make these by cutting various shapes from colored construction paper and printing, "B.O.T.S.S.," on each one.

Contest Emphasis:

1. To encourage students to invite new prospects to Sunday school.

2. To build an up-to-date prospect list in each class. Be sure to get complete information on all new children who come. Use these for follow-up.

3. To increase attendance.

Incentives:

1. For each new prospect that a pupil brings, he receives a coupon which entitles him to a free Coke (or free hamburger, or whatever you can work out with a local community store).

2. There is no limit on the number of coupons a child may earn.

3. The pupil in each class who brings the most prospects during the four-week emphasis will receive a special gift.

Keep track of the number of coupons given to each child. Award the grand prize at the end of the Sunday school hour on the last Sunday of the emphasis.

Definition:

A "prospect" is anyone who lives in the area and does not attend another Sunday school regularly.

Make sure the children understand that prospects are the only ones who will count during this particular emphasis. The prospect a child brings may be in any class and still count for him.

Promotion:

Announce the contest the first Sunday with lots of enthusiasm. The way it is presented will have a great effect on the results. Keep "B.O.T.S.S." before the children during the contest period by sending letters and making phone calls.

Blast Off to 1,000

Instructions to Pupils:

1. The contest covers four weeks and is for juniors only.

2. Start getting team members today.

3. You are the captain of your team. Ask church people to be members of your team. A person can help you only ONE Sunday of the four. You must get help from FOUR different people. Example: If you ask John Jones to be on your team for the first Sunday, he cannot be on your team for the second, third, or fourth Sunday. Ask someone else for those Sundays.

4. Any person who is in a primary class or above may be a member of your team.

5. The most energetic and alert captains will have the most members on their teams. So get with it!

How to Obtain Points:

1. Each visitor YOU bring to Sunday school is worth 25 points.

2. Each visitor that a team member brings to Sunday school is worth 20 points. Each Sunday, AFTER Sunday school is over, check with your team members to see whom they brought.

A score sheet MUST be filled out each week and turned

21

in by 9 p.m. the next Sunday, or you will receive no points for that day.

Awards:

The first-place winner receives $5.00 or $10.00 toward summer camp. Second- and third-place winners receive surprise gifts, such as a *Reach Out* Bible, a devotional book, or a picture.

Christmas Contest

To get the class Christmas tree decorated by Christmas Sunday, each person must work hard. When a pupil brings to Sunday school a person who hasn't been to Sunday school for the past six weeks, he gets to put a decoration on the tree. Also, the pupil and his friend get to select a gift from under the tree.

Junior Snoopys and Primary Hounds Contest

This is a contest between the junior and primary Sunday school departments. Make Snoopy and hound badges for the children to wear whenever at church during the duration of the contest. Each Sunday give five points for each pupil and teacher in attendance and 10 points for each visitor present. The winning department receives a free picnic.

Chain Rally

Extend this contest for two or more Sundays. In each department in the children's division the girls make green chain links and the boys make blue chain links. Each Sunday connect one link for each pupil present and five for each visitor to see which side has the longer chain in each department. On the last Sunday of the contest, chains from all departments are combined to see whether the boys or the girls have the longer.

Heads Up!

Assign each class a goal for each Sunday of the contest. Take a Polaroid picture of the class members and attach it to a chart with masking tape; list the goals on the chart. Plan special features in each class and/or department each week to create excitement and enthusiasm for the contest. On any Sunday that a class fails to reach its assigned goal, the class picture is turned upside down! Children will work hard to bring in their friends, so their class picture stays with all "Heads Up!"

Flowers in May

On a large sheet of poster board draw an outdoor background. Make flowers from crepe caper or tissue paper. Challenge the children to bring their friends to Sunday school. When a new person comes, a flower grows on the background sheet! Each week the children will watch eagerly to see how many new flowers will be added.

Cartoon Caper Contest

In this contest each grade is in competition with another. The divisions are:

4-yr.-old Bunnies vs. 5-yr.-old Birds
1st-grade Sylvester Cats vs. 2nd-grade Tweety Birds
3rd-grade Donald Ducks vs. 4th-grade Mouseketeers
5th-grade Charlie Browns vs. 6th-grade Snoopys

Distribute buttons with the appropriate cartoon figure for the children to wear.

Each class has a large attendance board on which to post its attendance for the day and also the number present in the opposing class. Door posters with "happy" or "sad" sides show whether the class won or lost that Sunday. A large contest board placed in the church foyer records contest results. Special recognition is given each winning grade every week. Children in each grade who bring the most visitors re-

23

ceive a gift. A prize is also given to each child who brings five or more visitors, and a gift packet is given to each visitor who attends. Department secretaries keep a record of visitors.

Telephone Marathon

What is a marathon? Webster calls it an "endurance contest."

What is a telephone marathon? A contest to see how many telephone calls can be made by pupils and workers in the Junior Department on a designated Saturday.

Procedure:

1. Challenge the pupils in your class to call as many school, neighborhood, Sunday school, and church friends as they can on the chosen Saturday. Calls may be made to any person, regardless of age.

2. Teachers should call all their class members on that Saturday—and anyone else they can think of!

3. Supervisors and secretaries should call all prospects —and anyone else!

Mechanics:

1. Place posters in each classroom the week before to create interest.

2. Award prizes to pupils in the department who make the most calls during the one-day marathon.

3. Provide pupils in the class with ideas of people to call. Furnish telephone numbers if necessary.

4. Call each pupil on that Saturday morning to remind him to participate in the Telephone Marathon.

5. Check with each class member on Saturday evening to see how many calls he made. Each teacher is responsible to tally the number of calls made.

Message: "This is a Telephone Marathon by the juniors at the Church of the Nazarene. We're calling to say that we want you in Sunday school tomorrow. Will you be there?"

Weight Watchers' Contest

This can be a one-Sunday contest, or it may be continued over a period of three or four weeks. Since it is the number and not just the size that increases the total poundage, many new children will be brought. Either have one set of scales at the main entrance or have a pair at each department door. Boys can compete against girls. Accurate records should be kept.

Poster Contest

This can be used to promote any special event in the church. Give the children the information regarding the event and set a deadline when the posters are to be turned in. Judges decide upon the winners. Display the posters in the church and various other places in the community.

Children's Art Contest

Purpose: To give children an opportunity to express creatively their interpretation of the Christmas or Easter story.

Procedure:

1. Set up rules for the contest—paper size and art media to be used, also subject matter.

2. Have the pictures judged by a committee.

3. Display all pictures submitted in a centrally located area.

4. Present suitable prizes to the winners in each category or age-group.

Christmas Story Contest

The children are to write the story of Christmas using all of the words listed below. Award a prize to the winner in each grade. All stories should be displayed or printed for the church members to enjoy.

A—angels	**M**—manger
B—baby, Bethlehem	**N**—Nazareth
C—camels	**O**—ox
D—donkey, doves	**P**—Prince of Peace
E—East	**Q**—quietly
F—firstborn, frankincense	**R**—Ruler, ran
G—"Glory to God"	**S**—shepherds, stable
H—Herod, hosanna	**T**—tidings, treasure
I—innkeeper	**U**—unto us (a child is born)
J—Joseph, joy	**V**—virgin, visit
K—kings, kneel	**W**—wonder, worship
L—lambs, love	**Y**—young (child)

VISITATION

Unless there are pupils in the class, the efforts of even the best teacher are in vain. If nobody is present, the teacher might as well stay at home. There is always a cause for the child's absence, even though we do not think it a sufficient reason. Whatever the cause of the absence, it is real in the life of the pupil—and should not be neglected by the teacher.

Cards and letters should be sent to absent pupils, to visitors and prospects, and to pupils who attend regularly. Special days and occasions should be remembered. But this means of contact is only 10 percent effective. Telephone calls should be made regularly, but at best they are only 20 percent effective. Personal calls made in the homes are 80 percent effective!

Do You Really Care?

There are many occasions when a teacher should visit in the homes of his pupils. Immediately after a pupil has been promoted into the class the teacher should show that he cares by paying a visit to the home. This helps the pupil to get acquainted with his new teacher, and the teacher can get to know the pupil, his family, and home surroundings better.

During the week following a pupil's absence, the teacher should visit the home. Knowing that someone cares about his not attending Sunday school will encourage the child to be more regular. A good idea is to take a copy of the Sunday school paper, so the pupil will not miss reading this vital periodical.

Whenever a pupil is sick, the teacher should visit in the home or hospital. And certainly the teacher would visit the home in the event of tragedy, such as death, in the family. What better way is there to convey the idea that you care?

The pupil who never misses a Sunday should not be denied the attention and care of his teacher. Visit in the home and challenge this pupil to do a special report or project for the class.

Whenever a new prospect attends the class, the teacher should visit in the home the following week. This personal interest may mean winning the new child to the church and eventually to Christ.

Invasion Week

Purpose: Each teacher is to visit in the home of every member of the class sometime during this week designated. These visits give opportunity for the teacher to meet the pupils' parents and see situations under which the children live. This helps the teacher to understand the child better and makes the teaching experience more effective. During the visit the teacher may share something good or interesting about the child, thus helping to enlarge communication channels between parent and teacher.

Follow-up: Share interesting experiences and insights gained from visits at the next departmental Sunday school teachers' meeting.

"Because I Love Him"

This special outreach program emphasizes personal contact. Each teacher is challenged to visit personally every home represented in her class during a month's time.

Progressive Visitation

This visitation time-saver has a dual purpose: (1) visiting in the home; and (2) individual contact with the pupils. The teacher stops by the first home for a brief visit; then this pupil accompanies the teacher to the next house. After a visit with the family in this home, the two pupils and the teacher continue to the next house—and so on until all pupils have been picked up. The final stop is for a Coke or other treat; then everyone is returned to his home.

Don't Forget the Regulars

A mother related the following to her son's teacher: "I just want you to know how much our son appreciates your phone call each Saturday night. He has always been one of the regulars and many of his teachers have just taken it for granted that he would be in Sunday school each week. He hasn't received the attention through visits, letters, and phone calls that some of the chronic absentees receive. His face simply lights up when the phone rings on Saturday night, because he knows that his Sunday school teacher is calling just to chat with him a few minutes. Thanks for what you're doing for our son." Teacher, remember those "regular" pupils need to know that you care about them too.

ADMINISTRATION

Open House

Possible Times:
1. Sunday evening, following dismissal of church
2. During regular Sunday school session
3. A night during the week

Participants:
1. Children's division only
2. Children's division and teen department

Objectives:
1. To acquaint parents with the church's educational ministry
2. To give children an opportunity to introduce their parents and teachers
3. To allow informal sharing of ideas between parents and teachers
4. To show results of the children's work and study:
   a. Bulletin boards
   b. Special projects
   c. Worship center
   d. Workbooks
   e. Unit displays

Promotion:
1. Send a written invitation to each home.
2. Talk about open house in the Sunday school classes.
3. Telephone all parents a week ahead of time.
4. Use attractive announcements in the church newsletter.

Other Features:
1. Serve refreshments.
2. Place helpful mimeographed materials in each room for parents to take:
   a. Child characteristics and needs
   b. Objectives of the Sunday school
   c. Coming activities and plans
   d. Outline of lessons for a year
   e. Guidelines for better church/home cooperation and relationship

Department Room Dedication

If a Sunday school classroom has been redecorated, remodeled, or newly built, plan a department room dedication service. An appropriate service would include:

1. Welcome by the supervisor
2. Responsive reading of Ps. 127:1, "Except the Lord build the house, they labour in vain that build it."
3. Group song about the church
4. A challenge by the pastor, emphasizing that the department room is their Sunday school home and it is to be theirs. He should urge the children to show their respect and love by the way they care for the room.
5. Concluding prayer by the Sunday school superintendent

Curriculum Center

Purpose: To provide teachers, supervisors, other workers with adequate resource material for their own learning and for their teaching.

Contents: The center should be in a room used exclusively for resource materials and helps. Included would be: audiovisual materials; maps; illustrations and pictures; comprehensive material on age-groups; files of clippings on varied topics; creative idea books for decorating, activities, and effective teaching; Christian education magazines; reference books, supplies, teachers' quarterlies and guides; catalogues; bulletins, pamphlets; picture files; and so on.

Operation: The center should be accessible throughout the week, as well as on Sunday. All materials would be checked out by the user.

A Worker's Handbook

One way to increase the effectiveness of those who work with children in the Sunday school is to compile a handbook to give a broad understanding of the overall program. The handbook should contain objectives, policies, and job descriptions. Policies should include such items as the procedure for giving recognition to new children, scheduling activities, training, visitation standards, record system, promotion, curriculum, class names, classrooms, audiovisual aids and equipment, visual aids, supplies, and the library. Job descriptions should be written out for the division superintendent, supervisors, teachers, and secretaries.

Workbook Award

To encourage superior work and give recognition that is due, give a "Workbook Award." At the end of each quarter, primary and junior pupils who have complete, correct, and neat Sunday school workbooks receive this "Award." A large seal is pasted on the front of the workbook and a certificate is awarded publicly by the Sunday school superintendent or the department supervisor. The certificate reads: "This certifies that [name] has qualified for the *Workbook Award* by having a complete, correct, and neat workbook for the quarter of [date]."

Children's Library

A church library especially for children will provide worthwhile reading materials for the boys and girls. The library will serve also as a resource for teachers in the children's division. Such a library would include books which give background material for Bible study, Christian fiction and biography, books to display on the browsing table for pupils to look at during presession time, and books which contain illustrations and stories to support the lesson. Pupils will find the library very helpful when they are asked to make reports or do research for a particular lesson.

What steps need to be followed when organizing a children's Sunday school library? First of all, the books need to be obtained. This can be done (1) by challenging each child to buy, as a gift to the library, a book in which his name will be printed as the purchaser; (2) by using funds allocated from the church or Sunday school budget; (3) by making an appeal to parents and church members to buy individual books; and (4) by taking a special offering in the church service.

Books can be classified into the following categories: Bible (general), Old Testament, New Testament, Jesus, God, prayer, missions, church, devotional, fiction, and biography. Compile a card file, making an author card, a title card, and a subject card on each book in your library. An efficient method of classifying is to use the simplified "Dewey Decimal System." Information regarding this system can be obtained from any public library.

Other items which must be decided are: (1) where the library will be located, (2) when it will be open, and (3) who will serve as assistant librarians.

A publicity campaign is a must. The library should be mentioned often in the Sunday school classes. An occasional trip to the library during the Sunday school hour will help motivate the children to read. A bulletin board just for the library should be placed where it is easy for all to see. Items of interest regarding the children's library and new books obtained should be mentioned in the church newsletter.

To function successfully, the children's Sunday school library must have rules. Here are some suggestions:

1. No more than two books may be checked out at one time.

2. Books may be checked out for a seven-day period.

3. Books may be renewed for one seven-day period.

4. Two cents will be charged for each day that a book is overdue. (Some set a weekly rate of 10c, since the children are not at the church between Sundays.)

5. If a book is lost, the borrower must pay for it.

6. If a book is marked, torn, or damaged in any way, the borrower must pay according to the damage done.

7. No book may be checked out or returned unless a librarian is in the library.

Bus Program

Purpose: To win entire families to Christ and help them to become established in a church home where they can function as effective, growing Christians.

Suggestions:

1. Duplicate a list of all children on the bus according to Sunday school classes. Include addresses and telephone numbers. Encourage fellow classmates to contact those who are absent.

2. Investigate the possibility of holding a neighborhood Bible club in a home in the bus route area.

3. Poll the bus families to see if some would appreciate a telephone call on Sunday morning to awaken the children in time to get ready for Sunday school.

4. Take a Saturday trip to the zoo or some other place of interest. Let the children bring sack lunches and spend the day.

5. Have a family picnic, potluck style. Invite church families and bus-children families. Plan activities for all ages.

6. Involve the parents of the bus children in the church's program. Make sure they are invited to special activities.

7. Organize home Bible study groups in the bus-route neighborhood. This is an excellent tool for spiritual growth and additional outreach.

Results:

1. More people are involved in Bible study and worship.

2. More individuals are won for Christ and the church.

3. Solves the transportation problem for those children

who want to come to Sunday school but whose parents are not interested enough to bring them.

4. Provides a place of service for more people; some who cannot teach can help with the bus program.

5. Provides opportunities for more effective, organized witnessing because each week parents and children on the route are contacted.

MISCELLANEOUS

Some Pointers on Publicity

1. *Attractiveness.* Promotional materials should look attractive. If the only printing equipment available is a ditto or mimeo machine, keep it clean and in good working order and publicity pieces will come out looking neat.

2. *Clarity.* Know exactly what message you want to get across and state it clearly. Check to make sure that all information is accurate. Say everything as briefly as possible. Organize your thoughts, so the material is well presented. Try to get a personal tone in your advertisements.

3. *Relevance.* People respond to ideas which are presented so they see how they relate to them. Be on the lookout for interesting ideas in newspapers, magazines, door-to-door advertising, mailers, and store windows. Incorporate these into your publicity pieces.

4. *Color.* Don't use white paper if colored paper is available. Don't use a drab yellow if you can use a bright goldenrod. Don't be satisfied with only black ink if a two-color job would be appropriate. Publicity that is bright and colorful has a better chance of being looked at and read.

5. *Unusual.* Don't do the same thing in the same way. Try to make your advertisements different. Be creative and adapt ideas. Give your materials a new look and your reader will take a second glance.

6. *Efficiency.* Plan all your publicity items ahead of time. Know exactly when they need to reach individuals

and when they must be mailed in order to arrive on time. It's much better for materials to arrive a few days early than even one day late.

Publicize Contacts

"Nothing succeeds like success!" "Enthusiasm is contagious." Trite—but true when applied to Sunday school contacts. Encourage workers who are calling each week—and inspire those who are not doing the job by trying some of the following:

1. Place a board in the foyer that lists each class in the Sunday school. Post the number of contacts made by the class each week.

2. Place an 8½ x 11 poster on the door of each classroom and/or department, listing the teacher's name and the enrollment of the class. Write in the dates for an entire month and provide space to post each week's attendance and the number of contacts made by the teacher and members. At the bottom of the poster write: "Watch our progress because of our work!"

3. List in the church newsletter the number of contacts made by each class.

4. In a public service, occasionally commend teachers who are doing exceptionally well in outreach.

5. Send letters of congratulation to teachers whose class attendance and enrollment have increased as a result of consistent contact work.

Really Listen

Sunday school teacher, do you really listen to what your pupils tell you?

Supervisor, do you really listen to comments from your teachers and workers?

Improve your listening effectiveness and you will improve your effectiveness as a Sunday school worker. Consider these ideas:

1. Concentrate on what the other person is saying. Mentally focus on the spoken words. Don't be guilty of letting your mind wander, with an occasional "Uh-huh" or "Hmmm" thrown in at random.

2. Let the other person know that you are listening. A glassy stare is a dead giveaway that you are bored. Don't do something else while he is talking. Don't doodle; and don't glance around at other people. Give him your interested attention. Make him feel that listening to him is the most important thing you have to do at the time.

3. Ask questions to keep things rolling. You'll learn things you've never known before which may be of great benefit to you.

4. Don't rush the individual who is talking with you. If he is slow with words, be patient. If he is jittery and up-tight in his speaking, relax and thus help him to do the same.

5. Agree whenever possible. If a negative point must be raised, be tactful and careful not to hurt his feelings.

Supply Summary

An easy way to keep track of material needed in the Sunday school classrooms is to ditto a form listing available material. This list would include such items as: absentee postcards, Bibles, birthday postcards, brads, chalk, chalkboard, eraser, construction paper, crayons, felt-tip markers, glue, gummed stars, gummed cloth hangers, invitation postcards, paper clips, pencils, scissors, seals, thumbtacks, visitors' cards. Give each teacher the list on the first Sunday of the month and have him turn it back in after checking the supplies he needs. This will keep teachers from having to look for needed materials and supplies at the last minute.

2. WEEKDAY ACTIVITIES

Reaching new boys and girls is absolutely necessary in developing a growing children's division in the church. Weekday activities offer a wide variety of ways to find new children, as well as helping those you have. Such activities are usually informal, but they should have a definite Christian purpose.

Afternoon Activity Club

Community Clubs:

The primary purpose of this club is to provide wholesome, character-building activities in a spiritual atmosphere for boys and girls of the community. Once the club has been established, the church can begin ministering to the unchurched children and their families. A bus route may be started from the club's membership; home Bible-study groups may be organized; friendship evangelism efforts may be undertaken, family nights conducted, and other evangelistic efforts planned.

Club meetings are held in the home of one of the lay families of the church. The Saturday before the first club meeting, leave an attractive flyer at each home within a three-block radius of the meeting place. The day before the first meeting, distribute reminder announcements from door to door. These flyers should highlight the activities for the boys and girls—exciting crafts, song times, Bible stories, games, puppet shows, and special features. Date, time, and place for the meeting should be stated clearly. It should also be made clear that the club is sponsored by the local (community) church. Use the back of the flyer for this message to the parents:

"Every informed parent knows of the moral chaos in our world today. In every way possible we need to develop in our young people strength of character. We feel that both of us have a part in accomplishing this.

"Psychologists tell us that a person's basic patterns of conduct and attitude are established during the first years of his life. The home is, of course, the center of this training. However, the church has always endeavored to supplement home training. We are here to help you.

"This year our church is sponsoring in your community an 'Afternoon Activity Club.' This program offers wholesome activities for enthusiastic children. We want to help them learn about Christ and His teachings. We are looking forward to enrolling your child in 'Afternoon Activity'— right here in your own community, at the home of one of your neighbors."

Careful records should be kept on each child who attends a club meeting. Include name, address, phone number, parents' names, parents' occupations, and the names and ages of all brothers and sisters. A notation should be made if the child attends Sunday school anywhere regularly.

Club activities each week should include a Bible story, singing, games, and crafts. Include an evangelistic emphasis frequently. There should also be special features, such as a peanut hunt, hat day, wiener roast, mini-treasure hunt, white-elephant exchange, backwards day, and so on.

At the start of the "Afternoon Activity Club" meetings, a children's edition of *The Living Bible* can be offered to the younger children and a copy of *Reach Out* for the older ones. To receive a Bible, a child has to attend three times and bring a friend with him at least once.

Kum Ba Yah Club

As a part of its total ministry, a church must relate to families in its immediate area. Try a "Kum Ba Yah Club," an after-school activity which ministers to the homes nearest the church.

Include in your promotion a letter to parents which reads:

"We are forming a 'Kum Ba Yah Club' for the children of our community. This is a non-denominational club which will provide interesting, meaningful activities for boys and girls—singing, story time, organized games, and refreshments. The club will meet each Tuesday after school; the church facilities will be used. We welcome the participation of your children."

About once a quarter, plan a program during the Sunday evening service and invite the parents. This may be the means of getting them involved in the regular services of the church.

JUG Club (Just Us Gals)

Bicycling, cooking, arts and crafts, gardening and hairdressing are examples of club activities suitable for girls. The organizational structure would include one expert leader with helpers as needed.

DAY CAMP

Most boys and girls look forward to summer. A vital part of a church's summer program can center around the day camp.

Definition. Day camping is a planned program of experiences for children in an out-of-doors setting during the day. It can be conducted at the church, using the parking lot or other available nearby space; at a local park; at a nearby state park or resort area; or anywhere else that camp-like activities can be conducted.

Director. The director has overall responsibility for the camp. His duties include: (1) stating the basic objectives of the camp; (2) deciding on the location of a campsite and becoming familiar with this area; (3) outlining a suggested schedule of activities; (4) reading the curriculum materials which are used; (5) organizing the publicity; and (6) correlating the day-camp activities with the total Christian education program of the local church.

Staff. Members of the local church who do not work, high school and college students, and professional people in the community are all staff possibilities. The counselors are with the boys and girls during the entire day's activities. If special leaders such as craft directors, recreation directors, and storytellers are available, the counselors are directly responsible only for the "Bible Adventure Time" and the fun time. If specialists are not available, the counselors are responsible for all activities.

Theme. Selecting a theme for the camp adds interest and provides a convenient way to name groups. If an Indian theme is used, the meeting place could be called the "Big Tepee"; counselors would be "tribal chiefs"; and the tribes could be named "Apaches," "Navajos," "Running Bears," and so on. An Indian drum could be used as the signal to stand at attention, a tomahawk given to the camper in each tribe who earns the most points, "tribal tags" with the name and picture of the tribe worn by all campers, and a paper entitled "Heap Big News" published.

If a space theme is chosen, publicity could contain such items as "lift-off" time; "passengers"; and "cost per taxpayer." Roll-call time would be called "blast-off"; campers, "astronauts"; leaders, "mission control directors"; the noon meal, "fueling"; and so on.

Using a pirate theme, the campers could be called "mates"; the meeting place would be the "deck." A "treasure chest" could hold applications prior to camp and then be used during the camp to hold gifts. Field trips would include "sailing" to various places of interest.

40

Activities

Roll Call. This includes flag salute, announcements, camp song, and roll call.

Bible Adventure Time. Activities include the use of curriculum materials (often the vacation Bible school study). The counselors are responsible for telling the Bible story each day, making maximum use of visual aids. They help the campers learn the suggested memory passages, and carry through on other activities as suggested in the teacher's manual. Classes are informal and are held outdoors to make it more like "camp."

Worship. The program should include both planned times of worship and spontaneous worship. (The outdoor setting will prompt the latter.) Counselors who are alert will find many times when campers can be led into a genuine experience of recognizing the presence of God.

Singing. Appropriate songs help lead into a worship experience. Singing also helps to bind the campers into a whole unit. Immediately after the morning roll call, for instance, singing the camp song helps each camper to feel he is a part of the larger group.

Games and Recreation. These should be well planned, have a definite purpose, and be supervised carefully. Appropriate activities include archery, calisthenics, basketball, kickball, baseball, volleyball, timed obstacle courses, and relay races.

Crafts. Materials found in the outdoor environment should compose the basis for craft activities. Possible projects are making a nature collage, a terrarium, spatter leaf-prints, nature boxes, and seed pictures. Photography is a good activity, and such projects as making bird feeders will be suggested by the nature setting.

Outdoor Fun. Various activities centering around nature study give the campers opportunity to use their senses of seeing, hearing, feeling, and smelling. Examples are: studying cocoons, flying kites, following nature trails, studying the growth of trees, taking discovery hikes, bird watching, plant observation, and so on.

Field Trips. Opportunities in a local area might include trips to a museum, art gallery, planetarium, synagogue, printing plant, newspaper office, zoo, dairy, or manufacturing plant.

Special Feature Time. The creativity of the director and counselors may be given full use here. Some ideas which have been used successfully are: Hat Day (everyone wears a hat, and the hats are judged in such categories as funniest, most original, ugliest, prettiest, and campers' choice); Peanut Hunt (peanuts are dyed with food coloring and points assigned accordingly); Treasure Chest Day (everyone receives a free gift); films; scavenger hunt; treasure hunt; Gold Rush (spray rocks with gold paint and scatter around); Balloon Blow (fill balloons with helium); Hobo Day; lunch hike; Indian lore period.

Lunch. Each camper brings a sack lunch. Drinks are provided.

VACATION BIBLE SCHOOL

The vacation Bible school is a strong vehicle in the church's ministry to children. It provides Bible study for pupils and a varied program that appeals to children. Workers are strengthened in their spiritual lives as they study and serve in the school. They learn to work together and to share burdens as they guide children to find Christ as their personal Saviour.

A vacation Bible school usually leads to an increase in Sunday school enrollment. It gives the church entrance into new homes and often results in parents finding Christ.

When the church shows that it cares for children in the community, people will respond.

VBS Newspaper

Possible Titles:
　　"Bible School Bulletin"
　　"The Superduper Snooper"
　　"VBS News and Views"

Suggested Features:
　　"Nursery Notes"
　　"Kindergarten Kapers"
　　"Primary Patter"
　　"Junior Jottings"
　　"Junior Hi Hilites"

Subject matter: News and items of interest from each department. Teachers will need to report for the younger departments. Select student reporters in the older departments.

Money-Raising Vehicles

1. Church banks. These are very inexpensive, so provide one for each pupil.

2. Henrietta and Alexander, the pigs. Girls fill one and boys the other. Weigh in pigs each day to see which weighs the most.

3. Two identical boats, except for color. Float the boats in water. The boys place their offering in the girls' boat and vice versa. The object is for the boys to sink the girls' boat and the girls to sink the boys'.

4. Provide a large fishbowl into which pupils toss pennies or nickels they feel VBS needs more than they do.

5. A "mile of pennies."

6. A penny-a-pound day.

7. Use old-fashioned scales to see which side brings in the most money in weight.

8. Build a church. Each piece of the church represents a stated amount of money.

Attendance Boosters

Shuzam or Zanzibar Box. Give a gift to pupils who bring three other children with them to VBS and/or who have perfect attendance. Put these gifts in a wildly decorated box to create interest.

Goldfish. Give a goldfish to each student who brings a visitor. A child may win as many fish as he is able to bring visitors. Goldfish displayed in fish tanks in each department will keep interest high.

"Brought One" Buttons. Give a button to each pupil who brings someone with him.

Mystery Names. Each day select "Mystery Names" at random from the VBS enrollment. Each child who is present receives a gift.

Crackerjack Day. Everyone who brings a friend on a specified day receives a box of Crackerjacks. Each friend also receives a box. There is no limit as to the number of boxes a child may receive.

Mystery Packages. Place inexpensive gift items in small paper sacks. Draw names at random from the enrollment. If these individuals are present, they receive a mystery package.

Surprise Money Bowl. Announce at the beginning of the school that everyone who has perfect attendance may reach into the surprise money bowl on the last day. Fill a fishbowl with pennies, candy kisses, and small trinkets. Children who qualify reach into the bowl and keep whatever they can pull out with one hand.

Ideas for Increasing VBS Enrollment

1. A parade is good, especially in a small town. It should be planned by the children and geared to children.

2. "Big Buddy Blast." On a table in each department display crafts, books, and interesting things which will be happening during the school. Pupils bring a buddy to see the display, enjoy a picnic, and have a good time.

3. Introductory sessions. These are held on the first two days of VBS. The object is to introduce the children to everything they will do in vacation Bible school, except the study sessions. Take care of enrollment procedures, and provide games, music, and a craft which the child can finish and take home. Do fun things these two days and encourage church children to bring their friends.

4. Pre-registration in Sunday school. One or two weeks before the school begins, have all children sign registration cards.

5. Hand attractive, contemporary, colorful flyers to children wherever they can be found—playing in the park, in the yard, or on the street! If possible, make a follow-up contact with the child's parents.

6. Sponsor a puppet show. Tell an exciting story. Create enthusiasm for the coming school by having the puppets tell about activities and by showing samples of some of the craft projects.

7. In your VBS publicity, announce a free gift for all who come the first day.

Backyard Bible School

This is a program of summer Bible study in outlying areas. Teens, college students, and adults are trained to hold Bible-oriented sessions in the backyards of selected church homes. Fliers are distributed in the neighborhoods preceding the Bible school dates. A sign on the front lawn marks the house that is being used. Children from the Sunday school may canvass the neighborhood.

If the first-day attendance is low, offer prizes for new

children. Plan an action-filled hour, using such aids as illustrated songs, visualized stories, surprise boxes, and puppets. Allow time for games, and serve refreshments.

Make a registration card for each child. Following the week of backyard Bible school, contact all the children from unchurched homes with a home visit. Place the families on the regular church mailing list for a year.

Neighbors react favorably to backyard Bible schools because they see that an effort is being put forth by someone who is really caring and sharing.

KIDS' KRUSADE

Purpose:

1. To serve as an outreach into the community; to locate new boys and girls for the Sunday school.

2. To provide a special, church-sponsored activity for the Sunday school members.

3. To give opportunity for boys and girls to find Jesus Christ as their personal Saviour.

Plan:

1. Prepare well in advance.

2. Publicize thoroughly:

a. Announce at least two weeks ahead of time in the church newsletter.

b. Announce in Sunday school classes and all other children's activities at least two weeks ahead of time.

c. Have the juniors of the church participate in a visitation campaign the week just prior to the big event.

d. Encourage all Sunday school pupils to take advertisement flyers and distribute them to children at school and in their neighborhoods.

e. Offer prizes to those who bring the most friends.

f. Mail a last-minute reminder two or three days before the Krusade.

g. Run an ad and/or article in the local newspaper.

h. Send an announcement to local radio stations for their church-news bulletin board.

i. If possible, put up posters and hand out advertisements at local schools.

Program:

1. The sky is the limit! Whatever you do needs to be sharp, interesting, and appealing to boys and girls. Possible program features are: singing groups, films, a magician, and puppet programs.

2. Secure an enthusiastic evangelist or speaker who can communicate with children. Give opportunity for an evangelistic appeal and be prepared with adequate altar workers. Have each seeker fill out a card for use in follow-up. Teachers and other children's workers should make contacts in the homes just as soon as possible after the Krusade.

KIDS' KORRAL

Plan a participation night on Sunday for all Sunday school children. Urge all pupils to come with their families and friends. Boys and girls participate in the service by ushering, praying, singing in the choir, playing the offertory, and presenting special features. The message should be given by using puppets or other visual aids. Give opportunity for the children to accept Christ as their personal Saviour. Careful follow-up should be made by the teacher of each child.

"CALLING FOR CHRIST" CAMPAIGN

On Sunday announce in the Junior Department: "Next Saturday we are having a 'Calling for Christ' campaign. All juniors are eligible to participate. We'll be calling door to door in the community, inviting boys and girls to Sunday school. Bring a sack lunch and we'll eat together when we're through."

Before starting to call, have the juniors participate in a 30-minute training session. This involves briefing, how to approach people, and prayer. Mention to the juniors several things they need to remember while calling: (1) smile; (2) be courteous, no matter what the situation; (3) you represent the local church to these people; and (4) pray in your heart as you work.

Give the children opportunity to get the approach question fixed in their minds: "Are there any children between the ages of five and 12 living here?" Consider the various responses they might receive and how to react to these. Finally, let the children practice on each other, so they will be more at ease when they are actually out calling in the community.

Divide the juniors into teams of two. Give each team a packet of materials and a block card indicating their assignment. Juniors will be excited after their experience of calling for Christ, so plan a sharing time. Children can be effective callers and they need this experience while they are young to establish a habit pattern for later life.

Mobile Puppet Show

Purpose: To reach neighborhood children for the church's bus ministry.

Plan:

1. Print attractive fliers advertising when the giant mobile puppet show will be presented in various neighborhoods.

2. Distribute these fliers door to door the day before the big event.

3. Decorate a car, station wagon, or van with tempera paint (which can easily be washed off). If possible, rent a loudspeaker system to play music and a tape to announce the coming puppet show.

4. Have the show in a centrally located area, such as park or school ground.

5. The puppet presentation should take only 15-20 minutes. It should capture the attention of the wide age-span of children in attendance.

6. Teens or adults should accompany the children back to their homes to obtain permission for the children to ride the bus to Sunday school.

Follow-up:

1. Obtain personal information from all children who ride the bus on Sunday: name, address, phone number, parents' names, age, grade, school attended, and so on.

2. Categorize this information and give it to the appropriate department supervisor, teacher, and other members of the church staff.

3. Visit in each home the following week.

4. The pastor, Sunday school workers, and church staff should continue contacting the "prospects" found through the initial visitation.

SUMMER SPORTS PROGRAM

Purpose: To provide opportunity for children to participate in activity that is both meaningful and worthwhile—NOW, during their formative years. Specifically, activities include playing baseball, basketball, softball, volleyball, or kickball in an atmosphere of wholesome sportsmanship and Christian principles.

Philosophy: Children have a basic need for vigorous activity—activity in which they are totally involved. A sports program may be organized to contribute toward the development of each child's physical fitness, motor skills, mental alertness, proper use of leisure time, wholesome social contacts, Christian ideals, and spiritual life.

Procedure: Each child signs up, stating that he will

49

abide by the rules, including attending regular practice sessions, and pays a small registration fee. Leagues are formed and games are played on a regular basis.

Summer Reading Program

From the first of June to the first of September, hold a "Reading Contest" in the Primary Department and in the Junior Department. Let boys compete against girls in each group. Make a large poster with books drawn on it. Each week the number of books read by each team in each department is colored in. The team which reads the most books is given a book to be placed in the church library, with an appropriate presentation sticker in the front. This contest will motivate the children to use the library more, and also give them something to do during the summer.

Library Club

Organize a library club for juniors who would like to learn how to be assistant church librarians. Classes should train these boys and girls in such areas as library supplies and equipment, processing books, and shelving books. After they are trained, let them put their knowledge into practice by having a regular time to serve in the church library.

Follow-up

The newly converted child in a non-Christian environment has a special need. Encouraging and helping him is essential. Such follow-up should include an immediate visit from the pastor. A visit should follow from the bus driver, Sunday school teacher, and other church workers who are connected with the child. The pupil should have a Bible of his own and an adequate supply of devotional materials.

Someone from the church should visit in the home

regularly to encourage and pray with the child, to answer his questions, to help him solve his problems that he is facing —and to witness to the parents and other family members. Helping the child to feel that he is a contributing member of the church group is important. Involve him in as many of the activities as possible and make sure that he has transportation to and from church if he needs it.

3. PARTIES AND PROJECTS

An Easter Social

"Who" Game. As the children arrive for the party, give each one a sheet of paper with mimeographed questions and a pencil. On the sheet are such questions as: "Who had pancakes for breakfast this morning?" "Who was born in the state of Texas?" "Who is wearing the color green?" "Who has a pet dog at home?" "Who has two sisters?" "Who has an *L* in his last name?" "Who had a peanut-butter-and-jelly sandwich for lunch yesterday?" Pupils are to mingle and find names to answer each question. A small prize may be given to those who complete their sheets.

Bunny Draw. Place several sheets of large butcher paper around the room, using masking tape to secure them to the walls. Divide the children into several teams. Give each team a box of crayons. On signal the first child of each team runs to the sheet of paper and draws a part of the bunny. When the signal is given again, the next child runs to the picture and draws another part of the rabbit—and so on until all have had a chance to participate at least twice. The pictures are judged on best team effort and most artistic.

Rabbit Race. The boys and girls get down on all fours and hop like rabbits to the goal line and back.

Egg Relay. Give each team a plastic spoon and a plastic egg. Each child is to run or walk to the goal line and back without dropping the egg. If the egg is dropped, it must be picked up and put back on the spoon before proceeding.

Egg Roll. The children roll plastic eggs by nose to the

52

goal line. The team member then picks up the egg, runs back, and tags the next person in line.

Shoe Relay. The first person in each team runs to the goal line, takes off both shoes, jumps up and down six times like a rabbit, puts on both shoes, then runs back and tags the next team member.

Musical Egg Pass. Children sit in a circle on the floor with two or three holding plastic eggs. As the music begins, players pass the eggs to the right. When the music stops, the players who have the eggs are out of the circle. The circle is formed again, the music starts, and the eggs are passed. Continue until only four or five remain in the circle. Prizes may be given to the winners.

Easter Egg Hunt. If weather permits, the final activity of the party will be to hunt for the hard-boiled, dyed eggs which the children brought with them. For extra fun and excitement include a number of plastic eggs with surprises in them. At the conclusion of the hunt, give a prize to the child who found the most eggs.

Easter Devotional. Tell an Easter story from the Bible, or relate an experience from a life situation that would be meaningful to the boys and girls. An Easter filmstrip might conclude this activity.

A Christmas Party

Christmas Toys. Write the names of toys on 3 x 5 cards. When the children arrive at the party, pin a card on the back of each child. The boys and girls try to find what toys they are by asking questions which can be answered only by "yes" or "no." When a child discovers what toy he is, pin the card on the front of him.

Christmas Charades. Divide children into groups and let each team act out something which relates to Christmas. The others try to guess what the group is acting out.

Merry Christmas. Seat children in a circle on the floor. "It" stands in the center and points to someone in the circle, saying, "Merry Christmas." The child pointed to must say, "Happy New Year" before "it" finishes. If the person in the circle fails to do this, he becomes "it."

Gift Exchange. Form a circle and give each child the name of something relating to Christmas—star, tree, manger, angel, etc. "It" calls out two such names. The children with these names try to exchange places before "it" can get one of their places.

Candy Cane Relay. Divide the children into two teams and give each team five small candy canes. On signal, the team members pass their canes to the end of the line and then back again.

Gifts. Instead of bringing gifts to exchange with each other, have the children bring food for a needy family, gifts for a children's home, or something of this nature.

Singing Carols. Close the party by singing favorite carols together. Take a few minutes to let children share answers to this question: "If you could have been anything you wanted on Christmas night, what would you have been and why?" Tell a Christmas story or show a Christmas film-strip.

Junior Department Christmas Dinner

Have a dinner or banquet for the Junior Department. Divide the pupils in the department into committees and let them plan the entire event, with assistance and guidance from the adult teachers. You will need these committees:

1. Food Committee
   a. Plan the menu.
   b. Recruit mothers to cook the food.
   c. Set the tables.
   d. Assist with serving.
2. Program Committee

    a. Secure a master of ceremonies.

    b. Plan a 30-minutes program to tie in with the theme.

3. Decorations Committee

    a. Plan table and room decorations to tie in with the theme.

    b. Take down decorations following the evening's activities.

4. Publicity Committee

    a. Design and mail publicity to all juniors and teachers.

    b. Make posters to advertise the dinner.

    c. Write up announcements to be made from the pulpit and/or used in weekly newsletter.

5. Cleanup Committee

    a. Clean off tables at the close of dinner.

    b. Sweep and put the room back into order.

Another way such a dinner can be handled is to have pupils bring the food. Teachers take care of decorations and publicity and each class can be responsible for a part for the program.

Great Pumpkin Panic Party

This is an activity for little "spooks" in grades 1-6. Each child wears a sack mask, made from a grocery sack. The sack masks are judged on: (1) most original; (2) ugliest; (3) prettiest; (4) funniest; and (5) most handsome.

Witches' Relay. Attach several sheets of butcher paper or newsprint to the wall with masking tape. Divide the children into teams and give each team a box of crayons. On signal the first child of each team goes to the sheet and starts drawing a witch picture. When the signal is given again, the next child runs to the picture and draws another part of the picture. This continues until all have drawn or the time is up.

Pass the Pumpkin. Children sit in a circle on the floor and pass a small pumpkin from hand to hand as music plays. The object is to not be holding the pumpkin when the music stops playing. Everyone remains in the circle. When the game is over, special recognition is given to those who have not been caught with the pumpkin.

Apple Relay. Divide the children into teams. Without looking (perhaps blindfolded), team members pass an apple to the end of the line and back up.

Spring Fling Thing

This is a new, exciting name for an age-old activity that boys and girls love to attend—a picnic! Perhaps the older children would enjoy a cookout. The children may bring all the food, or the boys and girls may furnish part with the Sunday school furnishing part. If desired, the department could furnish the food and the children bring money to help offset expenses; or the Sunday school department could sponsor the activity completely. For younger children, it is best for them to bring a sack lunch, with the department providing the drinks. Interesting games and activities should be planned for an afternoon of fun and excitement.

Hobo Hike

Ask the children to bring a sack lunch tied in cloth and attached to a stick. Hike to a suitable place, eat lunch together, have some special activities (such as organized games or nature studies), then hike back to the meeting place.

Mother-Daughter Banquet

This banquet may involve girls from five years old through sixth grade, or it may be held for a more specific group, such as primaries or juniors. Entertainment may include a special speaker, a talking doll, mother-daughter games, a mother-of-the-year contest, and mother-daughter specials. Any girl can nominate her mother for the mother-of-the-year award by writing an essay, which is turned in and judged prior to the banquet. These essays are displayed in the room where the banquet is held.

Father-Son Recreation Night

If the local church does not have facilities, check to see if you can rent a local school gym or the YMCA for an evening of activity for fathers and sons. Serve hot dogs or hamburgers, potato chips, and soda pop.

"White Elephant" Party

Each child brings a toy, a gadget, or a trinket which is still in fairly good condition as his "white elephant." The gifts are wrapped in newspaper. All children draw numbers from a bowl. When it is time for the exchange, number one gets first choice, and so on until everyone has received a gift. If a child is not satisfied with his "white elephant," he may try to work an exchange with someone else. Sing a few songs, tell an exciting story, play a few games, serve refreshments, and the party is complete!

It's Everybody's Birthday!

A party at which everybody's birthday is celebrated is sure to be fun. Try these ideas.

Secret Handshake. As the children arrive they are told to shake hands and say, "Happy Birthday." Two persons are selected before the party and are instructed to keep track of the third, fourth, and seventh persons to shake their hands. These children will be awarded a gift.

Pass a Gift. Wrap a gift using several layers of paper and ribbon. The children sit in a circle; when the music begins, the gift is passed to the right. When the music stops, the child who has the gift begins to unwrap it by removing the first layer of paper. When the music begins again, the gift is passed on. This continues until the gift has been completely unwrapped. Whoever has the gift when it is finally unwrapped gets to keep it.

Month Scramble. Make two sets of 3 x 5 cards on which are written the names of the months. Divide the children into two teams of 12 each. Give each child a card. At the signal, the team members scramble and arrange themselves in the correct order of January to December.

Calendar Relay. Use the same cards and the same teams you used for the "Month Scramble." This time give all the cards (mixed up) to the first person in each team. He passes them one at a time down the line to the last person. This player arranges them in order on the floor in front of him. When this has been done correctly, he passes the cards back up to the first player, who also arranges them correctly on the floor. The team to do this first wins.

Balloon Race. Give each child a balloon with instructions to blow it up and tie a knot in it. Divide the group into teams and place a chair in front of each team. At a signal, the first person on each team goes to the chair, sits on his balloon, and breaks it; then the second person; and so on until all have broken their balloons.

Days-of-the-Month Scramble. The leader says, "Get into groups of three." The children scramble around to form groups of three and sit down. The leader says, "Get into groups of five," and so on.

At the close of the party, sing "Happy Birthday" to everyone and serve refreshments, including a cake with candles.

JUG Party

A JUG ("Just Us Girls" or "Just Us Guys") party requires very little advance preparation. Ask each child to bring a couple of his favorite table games. As the pupils arrive, let them pick out a game they want to play, and the agenda for the evening will be set. Have simple refreshments on hand and let the children eat as they enjoy playing the games.

Bake and Eat Party

Let the children make their own refreshments for this party. Rice Krispie cookies or sugar cookies are easy to make. Serve them with hot chocolate after the group has played some games.

June Junior Jamboree

The purpose of a J.J.J. party (June Junior Jamboree) is to help reach unchurched juniors in your community. All you need is a large room, a garage, or even the church parking lot, and a little imagination.

Mimeograph a colorful flier with the following wording:

"Attention all JUVENILES, grades 4, 5, and 6. The date is JUNE 6, from 1 to 3 p.m. Ask your parents to get out the family JALOPY and drive you to a JAMBOREE. Wear JEANS or something old and comfortable.

"Some of the JOYFUL things planned JUST for you are: guess how many JELLY beans in the JAR; a JACKPOT full of prizes; JAWBREAKERS for free; JUBILANT singing; guess the JELL-O flavor; something for everyone whose name begins with a J; and lots of other JOLLY things!

"Be sure to have a few coins JINGLING in your pocket, for there will be a 'JUMBLE' auction. Bring a 'white elephant' (book, game, toy, or trinket you no longer want) and we'll auction it off to the highest bidder. There will also be JUICE (Kool-Aid) in a JUG (pitcher)!

"Tear off the ticket. It's your admission to the June Junior Jamboree."

To the bottom of the flier staple a ticket. The ticket

should include this information: name of the event, date, time, place; "Admit One—No Charge."

On the Sunday prior to the Jamboree give each junior a supply of the fliers and tickets to give to his neighborhood and school friends. Explain that the one who brings the most friends will receive a prize. For easier tallying, have each new child write the name of the one who invited him on the back of the ticket.

As the children arrive, direct them to the "Guess It" table set up in a corner of the room. On this table are such items as: sealed paper bags with objects inside, a jar of jelly beans, a piece of rope, and a dish of red Jell-O. Let each child feel the paper bag and guess what is inside, then guess how many jelly beans are in the jar, the length of the rope, and the flavor of Jell-O (without tasting it). Have him sign his name and record his guesses on paper provided beside each object.

Divide the group into several teams for relay games. Auction off the children's "white elephant" items. (Use the money to pay for refreshments.)

Award prizes to the junior who brought the most guests and to the winners of the "Guess It" game. Give a brief devotional and invite those who do not attend Sunday school regularly to attend your church. Distribute a brochure listing all junior activities for the summer. Conclude the Jamboree with simple refreshments, including Kool-Aid.

Junior Jaunt

This activity should be planned for early fall or spring. Locate an area which is suitable for hiking. Activities for the juniors during the jaunt include: *hiking*, refreshments, *hiking*, super song-time, *hiking*, sack lunches, *hiking*, film, and campfire. The jaunt could be done by an individual local church, or several churches could cooperate, thus giving their juniors opportunity to get acquainted. Suitable publicity should be mimeographed and given to the juniors so they can invite their friends.

Projects

A successful ministry to children must include opportunities for them to plan and work together. Every activity that a child participates in adds to his total development. Projects are especially useful in helping the child to enlarge his concern for others. Through working on projects, he learns also how to get along with others and the importance of accepting his share of responsibility.

Children Share Love

An annual tradition that boys and girls can enjoy is making their own valentines for shut-ins. Usually these are made and sent in the mail to various senior citizens. But the children will enjoy the project even more if they personally deliver the cards on Valentine's Day. The older people enjoy the visit and the children will always remember such an experience as a very enjoyable time.

Halloween Treat

Send your young people out in a "No tricks—we treat" effort at the time designated by your city officials for "trick or treating." In the weeks before Halloween, prepare packets of materials, using 6" x 9" manila envelope. Include a brochure of the church, a letter from the pastor (mimeographed on church stationery), a gospel tract, and a pencil. On the envelopes print, "No tricks—we treat," with black and orange felt-tip markers. Divide your city, or community, into sections and make assignments to the children. Have a driver for every two or three workers. Since this is done during the designated "trick or treat" time, most homes will have porch lights on and a knock will bring an instant response. Hundreds of packets can be distributed within a two-hour period.

Operation "Umbongo"

"Umbongo" is an African word meaning a present with which to express thanks. At Thanksgiving time children may being their "Umbongos" in the form of some type of canned food. These go to needy families, designated by the church board, or to a home mission pastor. This gives the children an opportunity to become involved with the needs of others. A reminder should be sent to each child during the week before "Umbongo" Sunday.

Christmas Card Project

Using pupils in the Junior Department, set up a post office in the church foyer. Announce to the church members that they may address their Christmas cards to persons in the church and bring them to the Christmas post office. The money which would have been used for postage is brought and used for a special missionary offering. The juniors sort the cards, stack them according to names, and tie them in bundles. Church families stop by the post office and pick up their Christmas cards.

Another way to promote a special missionary project at this season of the year is to have the juniors make a giant Christmas card and display it in the church foyer. Church people sign their names to this card and give the money they would otherwise have used to buy Christmas cards and pay for postage. The juniors should be on hand before and after all services to collect the money.

Witnessing Project

Handing out tract gifts at shopping centers makes a good outreach project during the Christmas season. Mimeograph, or type, a message on green or red paper.

Roll this message and a *Life Can Have Meaning* booklet together and wrap them in brightly colored Christmas paper.

The message could read: "CHRISTMASTIME AGAIN! And our fast pace of life becomes even faster with a December 25 deadline. Through giving and receiving of gifts, we celebrate the birth of a Child who during His life on this earth had some very interesting things to say to you and me. He said that He came to give us abundant life. He came to give life a meaning and a purpose.

"Are you satisfied with the purpose your life has now? If you are not, the enclosed booklet gives five steps to a new life you can have in Him. The Christ of the manger was also the Saviour on the Cross!"

Scavenger Search

Are you working on a presession project, class activity, or vacation Bible school craft that requires such items as pictures from old magazines, plastic bottles, ribbon, yarn, scraps of material, seeds, shoe boxes, and ice-cream cartons? Send your pupils on a "Scavenger Search" and let them locate the items.

Mimeograph a list of all needed materials. Assign points for each item—such as two points for each magazine brought in or five points for each cup of seeds. Give a list to each child and challenge him to find as many items on the list as possible and bring them to a designated place on a specified date.

An alternate procedure is to print a list of items needed in the church paper, alerting the church people that on a certain date children will be coming to their homes searching for these. Enlist parents to drive cars and assign areas for the "Scavenger Search" project.

Penny Panic

Let the group decide upon a worthwhile project, such as purchasing New Testaments for an inner-city mission. Give each pupil a jug or jar which he is to fill with pennies. Alert adults in the church to the project, so they will be prepared when the children ask them to help fill their jugs.

Library Project

Does your church have a children's library or a good selection of children's books? Buying books for the children's section of the church library makes a good project for the Primary and Junior departments. Here are some suggestions for collecting money:

1. Challenge the children to do without something each week, such as gum, candy, ice cream, and save the money for the book project. Each Sunday, or perhaps once a month, take a special offering to collect their "Do-Without Money."

2. Challenge the children to buy a book or books for the library. When they have saved enough to buy a book, they bring the money and a record is kept. When the book is purchased for the library, an appropriate presentation sticker is placed in the front, giving the child's name.

3. For younger children make a poster showing a facsimile of each book desired and the price. When a child brings money to buy a book, or enough is saved in the new book fund, he has the privilege of coloring the book on the poster. This keeps a visual progress record before the children.

Special Service Projects

Service projects can provide opportunities for boys and girls to use their talents during the week. Possible projects are: junior girls staying in the nursery on Saturday morning while mothers shop; holding services at hospitals and rest homes; helping the church secretary staple, fold, and address letters, bulletins, and the newsletter; doing odd jobs around the church; helping senior citizens with various chores.

4. LETTERS FOR EVERY OCCASION

Boys and girls love to receive mail. Letters are an effective way to advertise coming events, make last-minute reminders, and emphasize special days. But most of all, a letter says to a child, "You are important. This is just for you." Occasions for sending letters are many. Here are some ideas that have been used effectively.

Birthday Card or Letter

Birthdays are important for boys and girls. What a thrill it is for them to be remembered by their Sunday school teacher, supervisor, Caravan leader, or pastor! A simple way to remember birthdays is to make a birthday file. On a 3 x 5 card write child's name, address, and birthday. File these according to month. When sending cards, a commercial card can be used—but always include a personal note on it.

Secret Code Letter

This type of letter can be used to announce any project or event. The repetition involved in completing the code helps the pupil to remember the message. The Morse Code may be used, a code set up by assigning a number for each letter of the alphabet, or any other secret code you devise.

A VERY IMPORTANT MESSAGE!

Secret	A	B	C	D	E	F	G	H	I	J	K	L	M	N	O	P
Code	1	2	3	4	5	6	7	8	9	10	11	12	13	14	15	16

Q	R	S	T	U	V	W	X	Y	Z
17	18	19	20	21	22	23	24	25	.26

23 5   1 18 5   20 15   4 15   20 23 15

20 8 9 14 7 19   1 20   20 8 1 14 11 19

7 9 22 9 14 7   20 9 13 5   19 1 25

20 8 1 14 11 19   20 15   7 15 4

1 14 4   7 9 22 5   20 15   15 20 8 5 18 19

23 15 21 12 4   25 15 21   2 18 9 14 7

15 14 5   3 1 14   15 6   6 15 15 4

20 15   3 1 18 1 22 1 14   20 8 9 19

23 5 4 14 5 19 4 1 25   23 5   23 9 12 12

7 9 22 5   20 8 5   6 15 15 4   20 15

1   8 15 13 5   13 9 19 19 9 15 14

16 1 19 20 15 18   15 14   20 8 9 19

4 9 19 20 18 9 3 20   23 8 15 19 5

6 1 13 9 12 25   4 15 5 19   14 15 20

8 1 22 5   5 14 15 21 7 8   20 15 5 1 20

Prospect Letter

Send a letter to each visitor who attends one of the children's departments in the Sunday school. Thank him for coming, invite him to attend again, and list all the weekly activities for his age-group. The teacher could also write a letter similar to this: "It certainly was nice having you visit our class last week. I hope you enjoyed it. We have lots of things planned for this year that I know you will enjoy and won't want to miss. I'll be looking for you again this week."

Thanksgiving Letters

A. "God has given us a wonderful church to which we can come to worship Him. God has given us life and health. We can express our thanks by coming to worship Him. Why not be present in Sunday school for the next two Sundays?

"Why not share the story of Jesus with boys and girls of other lands who have never heard of Him? Our Thanksgiving offering will be sent to the mission fields to help missionaries tell the story of God's love for all men.

"Why not make every day a Thanksgiving Day? You can—by thanking God daily for all of the good things that He has given you.

"Thank you for being a part of our department, to help us express our thanksgiving to God. I'll be looking for you in Sunday school this week."

B. "This is Thanksgiving week, and we really have a lot to be thankful for, don't we? Have you spent some time thinking of all the things that we can thank God for? Did you remember to thank Him for sending Jesus to earth to die for our sins?

"Here are some scriptures which will help you to think about Jesus. Look them up in your Bible and fill in the blanks.

"1. The _____ of the world (John 8:12).

"2. The good _____ (John 10:11).

"3. The true _____ (John 15:1).

"4. This is my _____ _____, in whom I am well pleased (Matthew 3:17).

67

"5. *I am Alpha and Omega, the beginning and the* _____ *(Revelation 1:8).*

"6. *I am the bread of* _____ *(John 6:35).*

"7. *Unto you is born this day in the city of David a* _____ *(Luke 2:11).*

"8. *Thou art the* _____, *the Son of the living God* (Matthew 16:16).

"9. *The Prince of* _____ *(Isaiah 9:6).*

"10. *The King of* _____ *(I Timothy 6:15)."*

Promotion Sunday Letter

Promotion Sunday is always an exciting day! There are new names to learn, new teachers, and new classmates. Following the initial excitement of promotion, the teacher should contact each new pupil in his home. Prior to this visit, send a letter of welcome to the pupil. Here is a letter:

"I am so happy to welcome you to our department. Changing from a primary to a junior is a big step in your life. I want you to be sure to attend every Sunday. Be sure to bring the Bible that you received on Promotion Sunday. We will be using it every week.

"We have many exciting things planned for our department this year. We will have display tables and bulletin boards that you can help work on—parties—and interesting lessons. Come every Sunday, so that you will enjoy all of the fun.

"I'm looking forward to getting acquainted with you."

Christmas Letters

The Christmas season is a natural time to send greetings to Sunday school pupils. An original card is a bit more personal and meaningful than one which can be purchased at the store. Here are some ideas for letters which can be easily made.

A. Draw, trace, or mimeograph an appropriate Christmas picture. At the top indicate that this is a Christmas picture to be colored. Print a suitable Bible verse, perhaps one that has been recently used in the Sunday school class, under the picture.

B. Select a scripture verse that has been studied in Sunday school, and make a verse wheel, using a secret code. Draw an appropriate Christmas picture in the center of the circle.

C. Prepare a crossword puzzle centering around the Christmas story. If there is room, dress it up with appropriate Christmas pictures.

A Christmas Letter for Parents

"Hello, Parents: I think of you often as I teach your child. At this Christmas season, I want to share with you a few of my thoughts. Can you imagine a church without the eagerness of children—the untangled honesty, the curiosity, the wiggles and the swing of action and adventure? I love every one of them, and I am concerned that we provide the very best kind of program possible for our children.

"This month the story of Jesus' birth is fresh in our minds. Have you considered the earthly parents to whom Jesus was entrusted? They must have been wonderful people! Sometimes I try to read between the lines as I study the Christmas story, and try to imagine how Jesus lived as a boy. I think He spent a lot of time in the synagogue, enjoyed talking to His friends down by the well and inviting them to worship with Him, carefully studied the scrolls and came each Sabbath with His memory work complete. I think this was so because His parents trained Him in the way He should go.

"Even in Jesus' day, people were busy. But Mary and Joseph must have taken time to see that their children didn't miss the most important things in life. What a busy life we lead today . . . so many things to do in a 168-hour week. Is it expecting too much for parents to use a few of these 168 hours to provide religious training for their children?

69

"What are the important things at your house? What is most important to your children? TV? Playmates? Homework? Church activities?

"The children in our Sunday school are the 'cream of the crop'! They are well disciplined in the things that count —things that count for God and eternity. Thank you for your help in our common task—helping your child to become a firmly established Christian whose life makes our world a better place."

Reminder Card

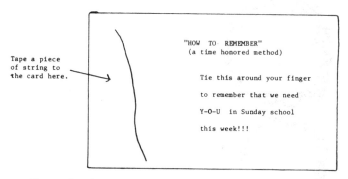

To make this card you will need a 3 x 5 index card, a small piece of string, and Scotch tape. Attach the string to the left-hand side of the card. The message reads: "HOW TO REMEMBER. Tie this around your finger to remember that we need Y-O-U in Sunday school this week!"

Summertime Letter

"Are you having a happy summertime? God has made many beautiful things to enjoy in the summer, hasn't He? He has made everything wonderful. Can you name these things God has made? [Draw in pictures to illustrate things God has made.] Next Sunday we are going to sing our thanks to God.

"Also, next Sunday we are going to have a birthday

70

party for everyone whose birthday was in July. Don't miss that! And guess what! Bonnie is back and will be there next Sunday! That makes us all happy, doesn't it? But we are sorry to hear that Doris and Patty are not feeling well.

"Now all the rest of you HURRY to Sunday school, because I'll be there waiting for YOU!"

Cartoon Letter

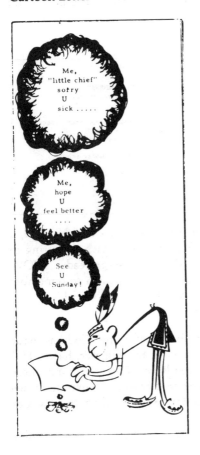

HEY ..... sure missed you at
Sunday school last week!!

Can I count on your being there
this week???
                    Your teacher.

Be on the alert for magazine or newspaper advertisements using cartoon figures. Copy these and add an original message which suits the picture. For example, a cartoon animal picture could simply say: "HEY! We missed you at Sunday school last week! Can I count on your being there this week?" Or a sad-faced dog could be used with the wording: "It makes me so SAD when you miss Sunday school! Please come next week!" A monkey swinging from a tree might call attention to this message: "Are you just hanging around doing nothing? Come to Sunday school. We miss you when you are gone." A friendly owl could ask: "Whoooo was absent last week? YOU were! We missed you! Come next Sunday!"

Illustrated Letter

Illustrated letters or postcards can be made by using stick figures or simple drawings in rebus style. Here is an example: "When you are not at Sunday school, I am very sad [sad face], and your class friends are very sad [sad faces]. Come to Sunday school this week and I'll be happy [happy face], and your class friends will be happy [happy faces]. Your teacher."

HI!

When you 🙁 are not at Sunday school, I am very

sad 🙁 , your teacher is very sad 🙁 and your

class friends are very sad 🙁 🙁 🙁 .

Come to Sunday school this week and I'll be happy 🙂 ,

your Sunday school teacher will be happy 🙂 , and

all your class friends will be happy 🙂 🙂 🙂 .

Mrs. Betty Robertson, Director of Child DEvelopment

Class Newsletter

A class newsletter is an excellent way to announce coming events, express appreciation to those who visited the previous week, send birthday wishes, welcome new class members, and so on.

Halloween Letter

At Halloween time draw a pumpkin on an 8½ x 11 sheet of typing paper. The message says: "Here's a friendly pumpkin saying: 'Hello! Hope to see you in Sunday school this week!'"

 WE **EXTEND** A BIG WELCOME

To Tim Talbot and Debbie Riley and Joe Garrison, visitors who registered

with our class last Sunday!!!!!!

Thank you all for your cooperation last Sunday in the RALLY DAY

at the Youth Center. We counted 15 regular members there from the

Banz Sophomore Class.

Sunday, November 19, is SOPHOMORE ROUND-UP SUNDAY.

All sophomores will eat Sunday dinner together at

O'Mealey's cafeteria on May Avenue. (It could not

be held this week because of choir rehearsal at 8:30)

LISTEN this Sunday for details.

DON'T FORGET. . .Thursday night, November 9, is TEEN NIGHT at the Revival.
Choir member or not, every teen should be there.

THIS SUNDAY...opening exercises will be in the church sanctuary with the Teen
Choir singing. _Classes will meet_ in the Senior High Department after the
opening upstairs.

 The Church Mouse says HAPPY BIRTHDAY to Mike Powers (Oct. 17) and

Linda Silvey (Nov. 17).

Novelty Card

Paste or draw a large black circle on a 3 x 5 or 4 x 6 card. Below the circle print this message: "BLOW ON THIS

74

CIRCLE. If it turns red, go to the doctor immediately! If it stays black, come to Sunday school this week! (Cut out the circle and bring it Sunday, and you will receive a FREE GIFT!)"

Regular Attender's Letter

Pupils who come week after week should not be forgotten by the teacher. What a thrill for such a pupil to receive a letter from a teacher or supervisor saying: "I was just looking through our Sunday school records and noticed that you have been present every Sunday for the past three months. Congratulations! Keep up the good work."

Upon Joining the Church

"It was such a thrill for me last Sunday to watch you taking your church membership vows! Joining the church is one of the important decisions of a person's life. I am so happy that you made this choice early in life, because the church can mean very much to you all through the years to come.

"Do make it a practice to attend all of the services of the church. Take part in its activities. Enjoy the fellowship of other church members and friends. Share in its projects. In this way you will feel more and more a part of the church and will be able to say, 'This is MY church.'

"I am proud of the way you are growing—both physically and spiritually. I want always to be your friend, and I hope you will feel free to come to me with any of your problems. My prayer is that you will always keep CHRIST FIRST in your life. Your teacher."

Easter Letter

"Easter is a happy time, isn't it? In fact, the first Easter was the happiest day in the world. Jesus came out of the tomb alive on that day.

"You see, everything in the Bible is according to God's plan. He made the world—and it was just right. He planned for Jesus to be born—and He was. He planned for Jesus to die for our sins—and He did. He planned for Jesus to rise again—and He did. He planned for Jesus to go back to heaven and prepare a place for us—and He did. He plans for Jesus to come again—and He will. Isn't that all good news!

"This Sunday is Easter Sunday. You won't want to miss coming to church. We are having open house for all parents. If your mom and dad do not attend Sunday school regularly anywhere, invite them to come with you to your Sunday school department. They will enjoy sharing with you our Easter Sunday morning activities."

5. CHILDREN'S COMMENTS

Children spend approximately one hour in Sunday school on Sunday mornings. In addition, the teacher may have some contacts with his pupils at church or weekday activities—and perhaps there are occasional visits in the home. With such limited contacts it is difficult to really get to know the children we are trying to influence and direct through our teaching—and through our lives.

Why not give your pupils opportunity to express in writing their thoughts and feelings regarding some topic? Creative writing projects stimulate children to think. They also help them to experience feelings of confidence in their ability. Choose areas of interest which are meaningful to your age-group and encourage them to honestly express themselves. Through evaluation of the responses, you'll get to know more about your pupils' needs—and thus be able to teach more effectively. Following are some children's comments:

"Dear God, how do You remember all our names? I love You."

* * * *

"Dear God, Hi! What is it like in heaven? I am very curious. Do You have dogs up there and how do You travel?"

* * * *

"Dear God, I'd like to tell You about what's happening down here on earth. There are a lot of wars and many people are poor or sick. Many people need Your help. We are having bad weather here."

* * * *

"I am proud of my country because of all the men that protect it. Someday I will do this too. I like my country because it is free."

* * * *

"I am proud of my country because it is a very nice place to live, and we believe in and want freedom. We have enough money to help other places that are poor and need food. We are a strong country."

* * * *

"My mother is a real necessity. She has a hard time getting started each morning but once she's started you just can't keep up with her. She does nice things all day and sometimes late at night for my dad, my brother, and me, and other people. We call her a real trooper. She goes to track, baseball games, basketball, football, picnics, camps, the farm (and sometimes breaks out all over from it). We also call her a pusher—homework, yard work, music lessons, cleaning rooms, manners, and eating vegetables. But she is also the best cook in the world. I could tell you many things about Mother but I hate to write. I love her."

* * * *

"Going to Sunday school is a privilege. It is as healthy as drinking milk and as G-O-O-D for you. It even gives you a BIG lift that lasts till the next Sunday."

* * * *

"Do you know who my favorite person is? It is Jesus,

because He died for my sins and He rose again. I love Him very, very much."

* * * *

"Dear God, sure glad You're around 'cause we need You."

* * * *

"Dear God, how big is it in heaven? Do You really fly on clouds or walk around? Do You have anything to play on? Is there a hole in the floor of heaven so You can watch us?"

* * * *

"Dear God, will You please take the smog away? You're the best Guy in the whole world and my best Friend."

* * * *

"I don't really know what my dad does that makes me love him so much. But if I get mad or angry at him, I can't stay mad at him for long at all. He does all he can to please me and never breaks his promises. I think he really loves God and trusts Him. I admire him so much because he doesn't drink or smoke, like so many men. I think he really is the best dad in the world."

* * * *

"I love my dad because he helps me with my problems I can't solve. He doesn't yell at me; he just talks to me calmly. Whenever I get into trouble he stays by me and helps me. He's the best dad anyone could ever have."

* * * *

"If Jesus had not been born the world would be in worse shape than it is now. There wouldn't be any Christians in the world today. I'm glad Jesus was born. The world is bad enough. We don't need it any worse."

* * * *

"Hello! I am a spide [spy]. My name is Coleen. I was at the scene when Jesus was born. It was very exciting! Want to hear about it? Okay! It began like this: Mary and Joseph had just gotten settled down in the barn when Jesus was born. A big, bright star shone very high right above the inn of the place where Jesus was born. Many animals were in the barn too: a donkey, a cow, sheep, and two doves. And now, you must have heard the rest."

* * * *

"When you think of Easter you probably think of looking for the pretty colored eggs that the Easter bunny left for you. That is what usually happens, but you don't think of the real meaning of Easter. Easter means that Jesus died on the Cross for our sins. How would you like to be nailed on a cross for someone else's wrongdoings? You wouldn't like it. So why don't we try to be better and do better things, so other people won't suffer?"

* * * *

"The Bible is a holy Book that God told men to write. It does not tell any lies—not even one-half a lie. It tells everything good."

DEDICATION

This book is dedicated to show you how to recover from a

nightmare relationship. Pay attention to red flags, patterns,

and warning signs. You deserve to be happy!

Mr. Ellis,

Thank you for your

support + for being such

a great leader!

Devon L.

Alive in a Dead Relationship

LIES. DECEIT. DEATH.

DEVON CHESTNUT

CONTENTS

I want to thank God, my Heavenly Father for giving me
the gift of writing and using my experiences to help
people!

I want to thank all of you reading this, for your support!
Thank you for allowing me to share real life experiences
with you regarding relationship red flags and warnings.

INTRODUCTION

Once you reach a certain age and still single, you get annoyed when people ask, "Why are you still single"? Another question that's frequently asked, "You're not crazy, are you"? Maybe you have heard the one that you are too picky. If you have gotten out of a long-term relationship, you could have been told, "You are never going to find anyone better than me".

Let us talk about the over 30 years of age group and still single. People act like you are a rare disease or a unique exhibit at the museum, with all eyes on you. Wait a minute and you have no children?!

Their statements become even more annoying. For example, "Are you sure you can even have children? How do you know if your reproductive organ can still perform"? Some people have the nerve to be so blunt! How rude! Tell them to mind their own business! Especially when you are out enjoying life and all of a sudden here comes the questions. You were not thinking about those things and now your mind wanders.

For the ones that have a desire to be married, yes, it is normal to desire a spouse. You should not feel as if you have been skipped over, it's too late for you, something is wrong with you, or get bitter because everyone else is finding their spouse making wedding plans.

The ones that are in a relationship but still feel alone, take an evaluation of the entire situation. Write down things you require in a relationship in column 1, in column 2 place a check next to the ones you meet, and in column 3 place a check next to the ones the other person in the relationship meets. Are these things that are fixable? Are these things you can withstand, for the rest of your life? Have you communicated this for a while but still no results? So what's the next step? Only you (not friends, family members, neighbors) can determine whether or not you are settling and the next steps to take. You have to be serious about your life and the people in your life. It was not meant for you to go through life and not enjoy it. Remember, you only get one life. Yes, your brother, sister, friend, co-worker may be engaged or a newlywed but do not get the sad face!

This is the time to be happy with them because you could be next!

Ladies, there is a gentleman out there that is diligently seeking you! You just need to continue working, planning, praying and basically continue your daily activities. When you take yourself out on a date, walk through that restaurant, movie theatre, or art show with confidence! Strut! Strong men LOVE a strong, confident woman.

Stop thinking that chivalry is dead! There are still men out there that open doors, pull out chairs, and buy flowers without motives behind it! Chivalry is not dead. It just does not go where it is not accepted. It only presents itself to eagles and not chickens. No, I am not calling anyone a chicken. I am referring to your attitude and your mentality. Do you have the mentality of a chicken or an eagle?

Chicken Mentality:

- Always clucking trying to out cluck the next person in the group to see who makes the most noise.

- Running around in flocks never wanting to be separated because your security comes from running with others that are like you are beneath you.

- Even if a new foreign chicken attempts to come in the territory, they get sized up to see if they are worth being a part of the pack. If they fit in with the obnoxious behavior of talking about one another, being loud, and wanting attention, then the pack grows. A growing pack with no mission.

Eagle Mentality:

- Walks in silent power.

- Not afraid to fly alone because even though the eagle is not seeking attention, the eagle always gets undeniable attention.

- Only associates with other eagles because they know their worth. It's not a cocky type of behavior because they don't hang with the smaller birds.

   It is a mindset of since they know they can fly, why would they babysit someone that can only walk? This hinders them from reaching higher heights viewing the world at higher altitudes. Solo but a huge mission.

You have to know your worth! Who are you?!

Gentlemen, there is a lady out there for you that will be faithful, loving, caring, nurturing, and submissive to you! Don't stop praying for her! It is not a loss if you have not found her yet. Continue to be molded into the king that you were intended to be in order for your future relationship to flourish! Women do not like to be compared to a former girlfriend, ex-wife, or your mother. Treat her like she is the only woman in the world. Only have eyes for her. Yeah, you may have your boys that you hang or chat with but guess what? Men can also have the mentality of a chicken or an eagle. It is not only women.

I want to question you, the one who is reading this book right now.

What is your mission (purpose) when it comes to relationships, based on the following?

- Friendship
- Dating
- Engagement

Could it be possible there could be a mishap in any of these stages before reaching the ultimate goal, which should be marriage? What do you do when the mishap occurs?

What about those in a relationship or engagement that have been together for enough time to have proof their significant other is cheating, lying, or entertaining other people?

Do you stay in the relationship because it's comfortable, you have that piece of rock that looks great on your finger, or to save you from being embarrassed from ending the engagement? Are you staying out of fear knowing they are not going to change assuming you will find no one else that would treat you better? Have you allowed a person to have that much power over you knowing the things they are doing goes against the true meaning of a relationship and you continue to cover up their wrongdoing?

In this series, I am going to reveal to you the mishap and mission of things I personally experienced. I am not ashamed or embarrassed to discuss it.

Yes, I was engaged and it just did not work out. No, this book is not about finding faults with others. I just want to share my story and help someone else avoid what I went through by seeing the signs but brushing them off.

I know you do not want to go through relationship after relationship starting from scratch learning about the basics. This includes what their childhood was like, what's their favorite color, what's their favorite food and so forth. That gets old quick! It makes you no longer want to date anymore. Pay attention, do your research, and do NOT skip over the warning signs. This book is not to bash anyone or expose my business because I am a very private person! That is not why I do what I do. It is to help someone!

WHAT'S THE INTRO LESSON?

- Don't ever let others make you feel like you are behind just because something has not happened in your life yet.

- Only allow an eagle mentality at all times. Remember, eagles hang with other eagles and chivalry loves eagles!

- Define your mission when it comes to relationships, at each stage.

- Make a list of what you desire to have in a relationship. Put a check mark next to the qualities you have and the ones you desire for your mate to possess. Let's be realistic, if it is something you currently do not have, do not be outrageous and place a check, for your future mate.

Patiently improve the thing you are wanting your mate to have so that when you have it, you will attract it.

- Do not stay in a failed relationship out of fear of not finding someone else, people talking about you, or being comfortable.

CHAPTER 1

Fantasy Love – Real Love

We all deserve to have a perfect future with the perfect person for us but ladies and gentlemen let's not be desperate. Ladies, if you are single and find yourself going places looking at every attractive guy wondering in your mind if that tall, toned, dark chocolate man with the fro is the one. Maybe it could be the short, caramel brown skin, bearded, bald man….yeah, he could be the one. Could it be that vanilla man with the goatee, sideburns, and a number 7 hair cut on the barber shop list? For the men, it could be that short, tall, slim, thick, dark brown, light, or toffee woman that locked eyes with you while the both of you passed each other. Stop that!

You're only torturing yourself with these make believe fantasy future husbands and wives. Now you have 12 potential, future, made-up husbands or wives that walked by and none of them are looking at you. Hey, I'm just being totally honest. Do not always mistake a hi for someone trying to approach you. Sometimes a hi is just that.....an innocent hi. You'll know if he or she interested in you.

I have to admit. I have had some relationship mishaps and once they all ended, I ended all ties because we no longer shared anything in common. What is the point of holding on to the past when I'm living in the present pushing towards my future? If I get to a point I know for a fact a man is not for me, there is no compatibility, or we would grow quicker going separate ways versus staying together, I don't hesitate to end the relationship.

Yes, it may hurt for the time being but which option would you prefer?

A or B ?

A)   Stay with someone that you know you are going to be miserable with every second of your life, day after day? You voice your opinion on how you feel over and over again yet nothing has changed. It's like you are a voice recorder that keeps replaying the same recording. Your feelings keep getting crushed as if a monster truck is rolling over your heart smashing it just to pick it back up, fluff it out to its original shape, just to flatten it again to dust.

DO NOT IGNORE THE RED FLAGS!!!

B) Be with the man/woman of your dreams who is perfect just for you! Every situation may not be smooth. Instead of sharing the details of your issues with everyone or stepping outside of the relationship, he/she resolves them with you only! I can compare it to this. His left hand would be named the atria in the upper chambers and the right hand would be named the ventricles in the lower chambers so when his/her hands wrap around you for a hug, you can then call him/her your heartbeat. That is how the person destined for you would protect your heart and have you feeling. Now that's love!!

Being a busy woman, working, doing community outreach, active in the ministry, in various organizations, working my own business ventures, the dating scene was not easy. "You are extra picky" is something I continue to hear often. I am very cautious of who I allow, in my life. My time is valuable. It is my life. I cannot afford to waste one precious second. Sharing my time with someone is like a gold medal that is won after a track race. It should be an honor for that person to know I freed up my busy schedule to enjoy some time with them. If it is like a gold medal, the man that I'm sharing my time with to get to know better is on the first winning block. He has the gold medal next to him because now he is in 1st place. The gold medal and 1st place go hand in hand.

Therefore, since my time is valuable I perceive and treat his time as valuable as well. Your time is your life. Do I want to be in a relationship? Absolutely! Do I have time to be in a relationship? Well, I will definitely make time as long as the person respects my goals, dreams, and ambition as I respect his.

I have had parents attempt to hook me up with their son. Even though their son was very attractive, I view the inside more important than what's on the outside. If the personality, drive, belief, action is not compatible with the outer appearance, I will not be able to move any further.

There were several times at networking functions people introduced me to someone who they thought I would "look good with and have cute babies". A beautiful baby does not mean a beautiful relationship.

As they introduced us it was a very awkward moment after the "hi". You could hear crickets chirping as we tried to find the words to say to one another.

Then, one time, I met what seemed to be like the all time PERFECT guy! It all happened in the supermarket. On a hot day, I pulled up in the parking lot to get a bottle of water. As I passed the customer service line, I felt a pair of eyes following me. When I turned to my right to see who it was I heard a harp play in my head followed by the xylophone and violin. I didn't know they made them like that anymore. There was this tall (6'5"), caramel, athletic shaped, handsome guy. As our eyes locked, we both said hello at the same time. I got my water and went in the self-checkout lane. Out of my side view, I saw him come up on my left and we briefly conversed. He was a total gentleman the entire time.

He asked me, "Why did I have to met you now"? I didn't understand what he was talking about and asked him to explain. He carried on to say, "I'm not originally from here but I have lived here for six years. I'm moving (miles away) to pursue my Doctorate to advance my career". At that particular time, it felt like the earth had stopped rotating for five seconds and I tilted to get my balance back. From the brief conversation we had throughout the next couple of days, we had so much in common, he was ambitious, had goals did whatever it takes to accomplish them, no children, one year age difference, loves Jesus and all 6'5" of him was moving in a few days. We conversed for about a month but then things started dwindling down. I was like oh well. If it was ever meant to be, things will come back around.

Yessss, please let this one come back around but even if it doesn't hey life continues.

After a while you get tired of hearing, "Oh, you're wifey material but I'm not ready for all of that". This statement equals run fast because he is going to string you along and the end result will be nothing but wasted time! What about this saying, "I'm going to marry you girl! You're going to be the mother of my kids"! This is told to you only after twelve seconds of meeting each other. Put some rollerblades on the bottom of your shoes girl and roll, roll, roll away! There is a difference between someone being sincere and someone blowing smoke up your tush because he thinks he is Mr. Rom-e-o, Don Juan, the charm lover that gets his way with the ladies.

IMPORTANT FACTS

- Stop having 15 fantasy husbands/wives in your mind especially when an attractive person says hi. Yes, the individual may be good looking but is their personality compatible with their looks? Does their character complement their outer appearance?

- Ok, so you had several relationship mishaps but does that mean settle?

ABSOLUTELY NOT!

- Some flags are red for a certain reason! It gets your attention. You have options so choose wisely. Options will be presented to you but that doesn't mean that's the one you should pick.

- You are a gold medal, a trophy. Everyone else realizes it but when are YOU?

DEVON CHESTNUT

CHAPTER 2

IT GETS DEEP

I have been single at this point for six to seven years. Someone I knew asked me if I have ever considered doing online dating. I have heard both sides of the story to online dating just like I have heard both sides of the story to non-online dating. Some turned out to be beautiful stories while others turned out to be the most horrific stories ever! I told her I have tried it once before years ago, for a couple of days, with no success. One site was mentioned and immediately I said, "I'm not with a booty call hookup site because I'm not that type of girl"!

She advised, "It's nothing like that. There are a lot of busy professionals on there, such as myself looking for something long-term". I told her, "I'll give it a try for a couple of weeks just to see because I'm definitely not having any success in my hometown". Before joining this particular site, I researched to see what it was about and made a decision to move forward.

Nowadays in the dating world online or

offline, many people do not do enough research. A huge amount of people do not take their time getting to know one another. Of course, you want to believe what the other person is telling you but you do not want to be so goo goo, ga ga, googly eyed that you do not notice the warning, danger, caution, and detour signals.

Have you ever had that time in your life where you could just rewind to a certain part, the warning part, and take the detour? Well, right before joining this site, the future me would have wanted this to be my rewind part. If I would have taken the rewind route, I would not be here writing this book to give you an eye opener on the DO NOTs. Out of a situation that wasn't so great came a great thing! It is this book so you would not have to go through what I went through.

At least you will be warned in advance or know the signs.

MY PROFILE

I created a profile, selected my name, and my headline stated this.

> *"God first and everything else flows. Jesus is my Lord and Savior. No hookups, no Netflix and chill, and no one night stands. Seeking long term only".*

To my surprise, there were several professionals on there. Keep in mind, I love marketing research so I researched them and found out the different ventures they joined. For the sake of protecting everyone involved, I will change the name of every person, in this book. I will call my ex Z. Why did I pick Z? You will see why later.

So I came across a profile that seemed kind of interesting. It was not a whole lot interesting but a little bit more interesting than the rest. I was trying not to be as picky as I normally would have been and saw it was a mutual interest.

STRIKE 1: SETTLING.

Z reached out to me with a hi. I responded back. Then it was just vague conversation back and forth. It continued for a couple of weeks. I was not at all impressed by this site or the people after two weeks. I got tired of it. In my last message with Z, I told him I am deactivating my account and if he wanted to stay in touch, he could e-mail me. He asked if he could have my number. I gave him my alternate number. After all, I did not know anything about this guy and he could have been a total creep or stalker!

Our first few weeks of conversation were through text messages. Then, one day he asked if he could call me. I advised he could. We conversed, he told me more about him and I thought to myself the dating site was not half bad.

FIRST DATE

Due to us living in two different states, I wanted him to visit me, for the first visit. He presented me with a bouquet of flowers. He was a total gentleman. He opened and closed doors, said please so I can go before him when we walked and I loved it. We went to a place where there were plenty of people everywhere and had great conversation.

Of course you know I had to notify several people of where I was going, his name, contact information, and the car he drove, along with the license plate number for protection. We talked about dreams, goals, and all of that good stuff. The night ended pretty great.

DIG DEEPER

During our getting to know each other phase, I did some intense, extensive research on Z. What did I find out? I found out with his job, he lived in several states, due to various contract assignments. Is there more? Yes, I found out about his family members. Is that it? Of course not! I found out that he was previously married as well. Hmmm…. When we got to the topic about his family, jobs, salary, everything lined up with the research I found.

There was still no word about his previous marriage but know I was waiting for the right time to ask.

We got on the topic of marriage one day. He asked, "Do you ever want to get married"? My response, "Yes". I also asked, "Have you ever been married or engaged before"? His response, "No".

Lie number 1!

I have already done my due diligence and found out he used to be married. I started to throw the cards on the table right then and there like I had the Big Joker, Little Joker, Ace of Spades, King of Spades, Queen of Spades, and the Jack of Spades, for all of my card players. For all of my non-card players, that's a winning hand if you play it right! Now, I waited for the right time to bring it up. Z beat me to it though.

He said, "I have to tell you something". I said, "Ok, what's up"? Z stated, "I have been married before. We were together for many years but were only married for six months". I told him, "I know". He was surprised and was like yeah right she doesn't know all of that. I told him, "The name of your ex wife is W and she was on your FB page three weeks ago but now she is no longer your FB friend". This blew his mind!! He couldn't believe I found that type of information. I told him, "Previously, I did not ask you if you were married because I did not know". I asked you because I wanted you to reveal the truth to me". For all of you reading this, did you know that even though you make your list of friends private, you can still see who is on the friend list? Yep!

VISIT HIS STATE

After several visits of him coming here, I thought it was only fair that I go visit him after I felt comfortable. He stated his sister that lives out-of-town came in and the rest of his sisters, mother, brother-in-laws will be at the house. He wanted me to meet them. I was up for it. First, we toured his old neighborhood, schools, parks and it was pretty cool. We got to the house of his family member. I met his mom, sisters, and brother-in-laws.

As soon as I sat down for literally eight seconds to rest my feet, he came back to the front where I sat. He asked, "Are you ready to go"? His sisters and I stated, "Naw, we just got here". He stated, "We will see you all later because we have plans".

Earlier before we arrived to the house he advised, "I don't have any plans just to show you around".

RED FLAG!

At this point, I became concerned with how quickly Z changes his mind. When it came to business he was like a Pitbull. He went for what he desired and didn't stop until he got it. I liked that quality. When it came to relationships or his personal life, his decisions always wavered back and forth.

Another stop we made was at one of the two churches he attended. This kind of concerned me because normally a person has one church. We entered the church and he gave the guy a handshake. The guy looked at me as if his facial expression was saying, "Aw man, what is this dude doing here? What does he want"? I chuckled inside.

Now, we walked into the sanctuary and there were three gentlemen that were hooking up the sound and stage. Z went in and stated, "Hey, what's up y'all? I'm just here to serve because I'm a servant of the Lord. What do y'all need help setting up"? At this time, I started to scratch my head because I'm thinking has our date been completed? He gives one of the guys a hand shake and said, "I'll be back later on to help". Did he go back to help? Nope. Was he putting on a front? Perhaps.

Later on that day he told me he was an active member of 36 churches. He joined churches while he was on temporary contract assignments, in the states he lived.

CAUTION

He picked a restaurant to go out to eat. As we sat down he said, "I'm really hungry, I'll probably get a couple of plates and desserts". I told him, "Yes, I'm hungry too". After we finished our first plates he stated, "I'm full, are you ready to go"? I'm really thinking to myself like what a minute bruh, you just said you were hungry and now you're ready to leave? This is like the third time in an hour period he changed his mind in a quick second! We left and I told him I have to get back home. The entire way home I thought about how quick someone can change their mind like that. It did not happen just once, it was like almost the entire day. Could it have been his nerves? Maybe. Was this a pattern that would continue? Who knows.

SIGNS, OH DON'T IGNORE THE SIGNS

- FIRST impressions could be FALSE impressions.

- Research, research, research, extensive, intensive research!

- If a man rushes you to meet or leave his family......you may want to take this as a sign.

- Just because someone goes to church and recites scriptures doesn't necessarily mean that God dwells on the inside of them. Remember, satan knows scriptures too and he is the prince of darkness. Some people take him to church with them every Wednesday, Sunday, all the days.

CHAPTER 3

RUSH HOUR

Z always made it clear that he wanted to get married and he was getting older. From the first time we met he stated he knew I was the one. I said to myself, "Yeah, I have heard that plenty of times before but you know what, we will see". I recall the first time he told me he loved me which was really soon. He said, "I love you but you don't have to say it back. Real love is loving someone even if they don't love you back". That statement had me scratching my head once again. I thought to myself how could someone marry someone if the other person doesn't love them back?

He told me he already told his Pastor he found the woman he loved and wanted to spend the rest of his life with together. In my mind I thought, he is not bold enough to tell me this about another woman in my face because we have only been together for three weeks! The woman he was talking about was me!

I thought this was too much, too rushed, and I take my time. I just told him, "Well, you never know what will happen in the future". I asked, "What is the rush"? He couldn't give me a solid answer. Z started to discuss wedding plans, having it at his church (I'm assuming the church in his home town and not any of them in the other states), decorations, and caterer. I found this pretty interesting.

DATE NIGHT

Every time together with Z now, I just replay the prior events that happened. At this point, I tried to determine if this is real because this only happens to people in movies….. right? Uh, WRONG! Pinch me! Somebody pinch me! Puhhhhlease!!!! Z told me he wanted us to go to the mall. We stopped at the mall and went to his particular store…. A jewelry store.

I began to talk and answer myself, with the following conversation. Me 1 said to Me 2, "Girl, he is not about to get you an engagement ring! It is not going down. The both of you do not know each other like that"! Me 2 responded, "Absolutely not, Me 1. No way. Just stay calm. We are in this together. Just stay calm and do not go through with it because this is way too fast"! Me 1 told Me 2, "Ok".

Z told the cashier, "Yes this is my wife and we have been together for four years and I want to upgrade her ring"! Me 1 and Me 2 looked at each other like huh?!!! What is the first thing the jewelry representative did? She looked down at my ring finger only to find no ring and no tan line! I just walked away. He asked her, "What's the biggest ring that you have available"? Me 1 and Me 2 are looking at each other now and begging on the inside for Z not to be a thief and have plans to steal this ring! He didn't steal it though. It was a beautiful 6 carat ring. GORGEOUS! I even had to take a picture of it. I had to smack myself because I was not going to let a ring get me caught up into saying yes to anyone or anything I was not ready to do. He asked me, "Do you like the ring? You are worth every single dollar"?

I told him, "It's nice". That was pretty much the end

of that conversation as we left the mall.

WRAP YOUR MIND AROUND THIS

- The words of people reveal EVERYTHING!

- If you feel pressure to rush into a situation, do not do it.

- You can not be bought by a piece of jewelry. If you feel deep down inside not to move forward, don't move forward.

- I have heard from people talking to yourself is a bad thing. Not in this case. Sometimes when I talk things out to myself, it all makes sense.

CHAPTER 4
THE PROPO-OOZE (PROPOSAL)

A lot of emotions are going on now. I listed the reasons why a man you have met in a short period of time wants to rush and get married so fast. I know love at first sight can happen and there are plenty of people that had successful relationships after meeting a short period of time. There are also people that have failed relationships after meeting a short period of time. He was so pushy in the area of getting married in like two months! If there is one thing that pushes me away really quick, it is to feel rushed.

DATE DILEMMA

At this point, marriage is all that is coming from his mouth. I felt very uneasy because the friendship stage of the relationship was totally skipped. We went from conversing getting to know the basics to him talking about getting married in a month. Huh? Z wanted to go to another mall which I was cool with that. I was in the shopping area and he told me not to come over to a certain area. I saw the area he walked towards and once again it's a jewelry area. Me 1 and Me 2 once again told each other he better not do it! He better not. So after I looked at some clothes I went over his area. He said, "No, don't come over here right now. Don't you want to look at some clothes?" I told him, "I'm done but I'll walk away". He came and got me after he was finished. Z had a huge car.

As I got in the passenger seat of the car, I sat down as my feet still dangled to the side as he looked at me. He pulled out this black box, opened it and I saw a pretty ring. Z asked, "Will you marry me"? Me 1 and Me 2 pushed each other and said, "Run"!

My insides jumped and leaped out of the car but my body and legs were still in the same position. Then I remembered, I can't run because I did not drive. I am not even in my home state! So I never answered and I stared at him as he stared at me. It was like I was in second grade again having a staring contest to see who can out stare the other person the longest. He placed the black box with the ring in it on my lap, pushed my legs from the outside hanging down, to the inside of the car, and he got in the car. My thoughts were what….just….happened……?

He started the car and said, "So, where do you want to eat"? I tried to figure out what went through his head like right at this very moment because a) He just proposed b) I didn't respond to it c) He changed the subject and asked what I wanted to eat.

Dinner was very awkward. We did a lot of small talk. He asked, "Could you wear the ring"? I said, "Sure". As I looked at the menu to see what I wanted to order, I could tell he took a picture of my hand with the ring on it. I asked, "Who are you trying to send the picture to"? He said, "To some family members and my homeboys". Z had already told some of his friends they were going to be groomsmen, in the wedding. He said, "I have 25 groomsmen". I said, "Aw naw, whenever and if we do have a wedding, that's way too many. I also stated, "I didn't even respond to the proposal".

Once again Z mentioned, "True love always loves even if the other person doesn't love". Now I started to think about those shows my mother stated she watched. Me 1 and Me 2 said, "Oh no, you will NOT be a statistic"! Every time I leave Z something replays in my mind on the events that occurred. I just could not believe this happened in real life, real time.

TRUTH HURTS SOMETIMES

Z told his family, his friends, everyone that he was engaged. Me 1 and Me 2 tried to figure out engaged to who since I did not respond. He asked, "Did you tell anyone"? I told him, "No".
Z questioned, "Are you wearing the ring"?
I said, "No". Little did he know being rushed like this was the quickest way to push me away.

He said he had a conversation with three of his homeboys. Z stated the first friend told him, "Yeah, one month is way too soon to propose to someone". The second friend told him, "She must have a dude there because she's not giving it up to you best believe somebody is banging her". Friend number three told him, "Just cheat on her and leave the females alone when y'all get married". I asked him, "Why don't you have a conversation with your Pastor, someone that is spiritual instead of your friends"? He did not have an answer for that. It seemed like he loved to hear what his friends had to say so he could make a decision based on their misguidance.

I told him I need to have a real conversation with him. I stated, "It seemed like we did an entire hop scotch and skipped the friendship phase.

I would like for us to take a step back and incorporate

that into the relationship". He was confused. He

didn't understand why I wanted to take a step back.

He advised that's fine. Now, he started to reveal more

things to me. Keep in mind earlier he stated he did

not propose to anyone and I found out he had an ex

wife. Now, he told me he went ring shopping with

eight other females. Eventually they all declined.

RED FLAG!

I do not care what anyone says, if someone goes

ring shopping or proposes to **eight** different

females, the females are NOT the problem! The

problem lies within YOU, the proposer! Then he

proceeded to tell me that his relationships were

always like two to three months, six months here, a

year then back to two to three months. A pattern!

Now everything came together. Insecurity issues, commitment issues, and fear of missing out because of age. Could this possibly lead to possessiveness? It could but I was not trying to find out! I am not that chick! Nope!

I am not at all for asking other people about the person I am dating because I know that is chaos waiting to happen. Little did he know, I knew about eight solid people that knew him, male and female. Some were even in his home town but he did not know that. I just kind of casually asked about him and I received the same story every single time. They all advised he falls hard for females super quick. Me 1 and Me 2 said, **"RUN"**! **WARNING!!**

TAKEAWAYS FROM THIS CHAPTER

- Do not skip the friendship phase.

- Do not skip the friendship phase.

- Do not skip the friendship phase.

- To get sound advice, sometimes you may have to go to other people that tell you what you need to hear. Trustworthy people! Sometimes those trustworthy people are not your friends.

- Patterns are important! Don't ignore patterns.

- Do not skip the friendship phase.

DEVON CHESTNUT

CHAPTER 5

INFORMATION CAN

FALL IN YOUR LAP

I replayed everything in my head. Now that we have backed up to the friendship phase, he told me stuff left and right. Stuff that I should have known at the beginning. On this day, I had a meeting with my Spiritual Mother and some other ladies just to discuss about dating. I still had two hours before the meeting took place. All of a sudden, my phone rings. It is Z. I answered and he accidentally pocket dialed me. I yelled, sent texts, switched over to the other line and called him repeatedly because I wanted to get him off of my line. None of that worked.

Evidently all of those attempts did not work for a reason so I listened in on the conversation.

The first several calls he took were business calls. I thought to myself he better not cause me to miss one of my business calls. The very last call was like a gold mine. This last call sounded like a call from somebody he was real close to. The only thing I could hear was the response of Z. First he said, "I'm trying to be loyal with one woman and y'all keep throwing chicks my way. I'm ready to settle down and throw these other chicks away for good". He responded again, "Aw for real? She has a small waist and a big butt? Does she like to wear high heels? She has two kids? Mannn naw! Y'all quit trying to hook me up".

Next I heard, "Man, I met this bad chick in Louisville and I'm really feeling her. I brought her a ring and she ain't even wearing it?

Do you know how many chicks out here would appreciate a real diamond ring and wear it?".

He then told him, "Man, I have to tell you something and I swear if you tell anyone, I'm going to fight you! I love her. That's why I brought her that ring and I want to marry her but she won't even wear it". After that he stated, "Yeah, I think she is messing with someone in her hometown because who gets a ring and not even wear it? Even when we are together, she can just pretend like she has been wearing it".

After I heard this the first thing that came to my mind was something we discussed. We told one another if there is ever an issue in our relationship, we will discuss it only with each other and come up with a solution. He violated that trust. The nerve! How could he? Why would he bring others into OUR relationship??!

The entire time, I had to text him every single word he told his friend, on the phone.

Every....single...word!!!!

I proceeded to go to the scheduled meeting and turn my phone on silent. The entire meeting I thought to myself how could he do this? It was wrong on so many levels! The meeting was awesome and very helpful. I already knew at red flag 2 he was not someone I wanted to spend the rest of my life with back then. Now, the accidental call confirmed it especially after he discussed with someone else about how he really felt about the situation. I never met any of his friends. What if he told his friends some information in the future? If we did get married, what if his friend tried to use that to get close to me? He did not think.

GAME TIME? LET'S PLAY

After the meeting, I checked my phone. I had 20 missed calls and texts from Z. Some of the texts stated, "How could you cheat on me"? "I think these texts were meant for someone else"? "Are you seeing someone else there"? When I called back I explained what happened as I tried to get him off my phone. I told him I sent a text of every single word I heard him say on the phone to him. What was the response of Z? He had the guts to say, "Naw, that wasn't me". Me 1 and Me 2 are like......REALLLLLY?? Do you think we are actually going to fall for that? Oh yeah, somehow the cellular companies crossed lines and put your number on my cell phone, with someone who sounds exactly like you with the same situation and circumstance????? Let's get real!

Z then said, "Well, if you could not get me off of the line, you should have taken your battery out to hang up and restart the phone". I told Z, "Aw, but I thought it wasn't you though". He was silent.

A silent, liar who is used to women caving in to his every fabricated lie resulting in him getting his way encouraging this behavior. Not this one. Never will I let a man, especially the man I'm dating run any type of games on me. No, I will not be humiliated when I had all of the proof. Guess what?? I did not even have to spend time to research it! The proof came to me! Look at that!

BUSTED!

IT HAPPENS

- When someone tells on themselves and you call them out on it, don't have them attempt to reverse it on you like you are in the wrong.

- Some things fall in your lap without you having to do anything except listen.

- You hear in your relationship, "If there is an issue I will discuss the solution with you only". When the issue comes up, they discuss with everyone except you. Heck, you didn't know there was an issue. This is a sign that future problems could end up on the local news station for the world to know. Everyone except you.

CHAPTER 6

WHERE IS THE LOYALTY

Now all of a sudden, Z wanted to research me and started asking me questions. All of that is fine because I had nothing to hide. The trust level was literally almost down to the single digits now. I always told him whenever I asked him something, 95% of the time, it's not because I did not know. It is because I know and I want him to be truthful. I asked Z if he had any other profiles on other dating sites. He advised no. Interesting statement considering the fact that I have already done more research. It was an odd name he used from when we were first getting to know one another. I wrote it down because it was not usual but at the time I didn't know the reason.

I researched the name and his profile surfaced. I thought that it could possibly be an older file that maybe he forgot to delete. With his honesty level being less than great, I took it upon myself to receive the real answer. Yes, I went there. If I would not have been lied to so many times, I would have not gone there. Where did I go? I created a fake profile on the site his username popped up and reached out to him. Catfished by the person you are engaged to? Sigh....

At the time, he did not have a picture up, on the site. I sent a message stating I liked his page. Eleven days later he responded with a picture being displayed, on his profile. This is while we were engaged! He entertained another female! I wanted to let the conversation continue and after a while present him with a surprise visit from this made up profile person, which would have been me.

I just could not allow that to go on any longer because that was hurtful.

I called him and we started to talk about different things. I asked him one more time if he had a dating profile he was not aware of and possibly forgot to delete. His response, "No". As our conversation continued, I screenshot the profile of the "lady" he responded to on the dating website. I asked him, "Did you get the text I just sent"? I knew he did because our phones were through the same company and he didn't take off the notification that showed it was read. He said, "Yes". I asked him, "Why weren't you honest with me? If you would have told me that you possibly had some profiles that you weren't for certain they were deactivated, I would have been fine with that.

To flat out say no AND entertain other women, that was totally unacceptable and I will not tolerate it". Do you know the response I received? He said, "My ex still has my password and it could have been one of them that responded". I told him, "Since all of them have your password, give me your password so I can deactivate your account". Ooooh, weee, he did not want to give me that password!! He stated, "Maybe I can find it in my office or maybe I can do a forgot password". I said, 'NO! Since your ex knows your password and "she" responded to the message, GIVE ME YOUR PASSWORD SO I CAN SHUT DOWN YOUR ACCOUNT"! The entire time I can hear him typing over the phone and all of a sudden he had access. Ummm hmmm… Yeah, he miraculously gained access to his account. Oh, and he did delete it because I checked. So much for loyalty!

Me 1 and Me 2 said, "Z, come on dude. Did you think you were messing with a rookie"? I'm always ahead of the game. Even when I'm not looking for information, every single time it always drops in my lap. Always! I guess you can say information and I are best friends!

INFORMATION HANDED TO ME

- Like the old saying goes, "You don't have to lie to kick it".

- This is a no rookie zone.

- I can smell disloyal people even from another state. I may not let you be aware that I know at the time but Devon knows.

CHAPTER 7

SOCIAL MEDIA NO NO's

I always knew deep down inside, he entertained females on social media but I could not prove it until now. On FB, he posted our engagement video and pictures of us, which is fine. I was not concerned about his FB. I wanted to know what was going on with his Instagram. I knew for a fact some things were going down on his IG. Most times when women feel that, they are always right! Of course he would not tell me though.

One time, he had an issue with me being friends with a male I used to date. Out of respect and to keep the peace, I deleted him.

Then, I asked Z, "Are you friends with any of your ex girlfriends on social media"? He said, "Yes". Me 1 and Me 2 were appalled! Even though he blocked his friends list, I got a huge list of females on his page and we went down the list one by one. The conversation went like this.

Me: Girl X, is this your ex?

Z: Yes.

Me: Delete her

Me: Girl, M, is this your ex?

Z: No

Me: How do you know her?

Z: He explains.

Me: Ok, she can stay (knowing in the back of my mind he's probably lying)

This went on until the list was completed, for that day. I told him we will pick up in a couple of days and then we will tackle that Instagram. He kind of got shook when I mentioned that Instagram page.

Then, Z started to send friend requests to men I knew on my social media page but he never met. This was his attempt to see if I talked to any of them. This was not just a couple of people, this was done to several people! To me this screamed RED FLAG! I refused to live a lifestyle like this with someone. With me, no one has to wonder if I am sneaking around going behind your back. Before it ever gets to that point, I am ending the relationship. Evidently what was once there was no longer there. Again, I have absolutely nothing to hide.

Any information he wanted to find out about any of my male social media friends, he should have gone straight to the source, which is me.

No relationship should have to go through this. This relationship made me exhausted only after three months. No woman or man should ever have to go through this. He told me no one has ever gone to the extreme like I have with the research. I told him I'm not those other women. I need to know what I'm getting myself into because I have to protect myself. I had to because he did not protect me. He thought he could get stuff by me but not on my watch while I'm the watch person. I have to admit, I will take some of the blame for accepting being rushed and not exiting after the first couple of warnings. That is so not my style.

I still think I selected the wrong major in college!!

Yes, marketing was right on but I should have added

Private Investigator! Hmmmm…..

WHAT TO TAKE AWAY FROM THIS?

- If you feel deep down inside beyond your skin, beyond your muscles, beyond your bones someone is hiding something, you may be on to something.

- A relationship can not be one sided or biased. You may as well be in a relationship by yourself.

- Information straight from the source is everything if they are telling you the truth. It's everything even if it's a lie.

- You may find out you would make an excellent private investigator. (smile)

CHAPTER 8

DANGER: I NO LONGER CARE

At this point, I am literally mentally done. Z visited me and we hung out at a park. He heads home and I received a phone call. He asked, "Did I leave my phone in your car". I searched and advised, "No, I don't see anything". He stopped by and we searched the street and the car but found nothing. I told him, "Give me your phone and I will call it to see if it rings". He gave me his phone and I entered in the first few numbers. I found it odd that he did not save his own number in his other phone. Then I thought maybe it is because he knows it. I started to type in my number in his phone.

My number was saved but it did not have my name saved along with it. If you are engaged to someone, wouldn't you have their name, a nickname, or something saved with their number? I temporarily set aside the mission and called his phone. I viewed the first few numbers in his phonebook. I found it very suspicious only numbers were saved with no names.

DANGER!!!

Normally I would question the reason for this but I no longer cared. My case was stacked up with enough evidence and I knew for a fact I could not live the rest of my life like this. I dialed his number and heard no ring. He got on the road and headed home. I did another search later as I really looked in the small cracks and found his phone.

At this point, I did not even bother to guess any passwords, what was stored or any of that. It got to the point everything in the relationship was getting extreme. I needed to keep my sanity and refused to allow a human being to take my joy or get me off course. It was just a distraction.

I mailed his phone back to him. The next thing I'm about to tell you is something I have always done in the beginning of a relationship. This was my fault for it being overlooked being so excited after almost seven years, I finally was in a relationship. I prayed about him and the relationship. Instant revelation was dropped in my spirit. Even though I did not know specifically what would happen or what was going on secretly, I had to obey God and depart from Z PERMANENTLY. God always knows what is best.

OBEDIENCE….the key word is obedience.

As soon as I knew this relationship was not the right one for me, I had to end it. I wanted to end it peacefully. Even though we did have great times together, when ever the "not so good" outweighed the "good", then that is a sure sign to LET IT GO.

KEY POINTS

- Once you are mentally done, you are pretty much fully done. There is no turning back.

- Hundreds of numbers saved in the phone but not one has a name on it equals something is not right.

- Prayer in a relationship is EVERYTHING! Not doing it could cost you your life. Doing it can save your life.

CHAPTER 9

SO LONG! BYE NOW!

Due to us living in separate states, I wanted to end the relationship face-to-face. I chose to do so through a phone application. Z already knew what was about to happen and he just told me to get straight to it. I wanted to look him in his eyes as I told him but I could not focus. His eyes kept shifting looking around left, right, at the phone then left, right and behind him. I asked, "Are you ok? Is someone after you"? He said, "Yeah, I'm fine, I just have to always stay alert and pay attention to my surroundings". I continued to talk. I told him how I felt about everything and he took it easier than expected.

He stated, "I knew you were going to end it with me that's why previously I kept saying, if we break up or when we break up". He knew the three words he always said that made me cringe were "if, maybe, and try". To me, those are not guarantee words when it comes to a relationship. Z also stated, "This is fine, it has happened to me several times before". If you could have been a bumblebee to see the like on my face! It was a look of shock and wow!

I told him I would mail the ring back to him. He said, "No, you can keep it". I said to myself absolutely not because I do not want that to be an excuse to try to remain in contact with me. I mailed the ring and took pictures for my records for future references. Then, the next day he told me he was tripping and to mail the ring back to him with the box included.

I already mailed the ring but threw the box away a long time ago. Me 1 and Me 2 wondered, "Hmmm, so is he trying to propose to lady number 10 with the same ring and box?! Hope she wears a size 7"!

I felt so much at peace! Oh, yes, so much peace now! I decided to block him from my phone and all social media! Three days after I ended the relationship, guess who updated their profile picture with him and another female? You got it! Z! Me 1 and Me 2 said, "Yesssss, girl!!!! Marry him now, please"! I was so happy to see him with someone else even after three days of ending it! I hoped she was a size 7 ring and they got married IMMEDIATELY! If they did not marry, I would happily find someone that he could marry! This is truth!

Even though we departed ways, I prayed for him. No seriously, for real prayer. I prayed that whatever it was that he was lacking that he found in Jesus. A prayer that he would have his heart changed, he learned patience instead of being rushed, and that God will send him the right woman when he is totally in tune with Him only. I truly do want Z to find true love. Overall, he wasn't a bad person. It was just several qualities and characteristics he displayed that were bad.

IT CAME DOWN TO THE FINAL POINTS

- Break-ups do not always feel good but doing the right thing sometimes does not feel good.

- No person or situation is worth your peace!

- Blocking the past is not a bad thing just don't run back to it.

CONCLUSION

I hope this book has helped you! The number one thing I want you to get out of this is regardless of how long you have been single or engaged, do not rush the process! Do not allow the other person to rush you because of their agenda, open or hidden. You can save yourself a lifetime of heartache by paying attention to ALL signs. Do not brush a single one off. If the signs start to become a pattern, you may want to re-evaluate the relationship.

Did Z have potential? Absolutely! If I waited around for the potential to be unwrapped, who knows what else would have been revealed!

I was not trying to wait to find out after all of the occurrences especially with all of the supporting evidence.

Sometimes we as women and even men are so busy being strong for others that when it comes to a situation like this, we need to be strong for ourselves! Did it hurt a little bit as I found bits and pieces of information? Absolutely! I would have been more hurt to put a blindfold on my eyes and continue to welcome this behavior.

In a relationship, I need for my man to be upfront instead of lying trying to cover his tracks assuming I will never find out. Lying is one of my pet peeves. I can not deal with a liar.

The same strength I had to overcome this situation, if you are going through something similar and are dating or engaged, you have the same strength as well. You may say, "Well you were only together for three months, it was easy to end it for you"!

Let me tell you about a previous relationship. I knew a gentleman for over 10 years but we dated only 6 months. He was pretty awesome. It ended due to major differences that weren't revealed during the 10 year friendship. It was not easy. I healed though. You can heal!

You owe that much to yourself. Don't worry about not being able to find someone else or someone not being able to love you due to the emotional scars. There is someone out there that will love you even more!

You will look back at your past relationship and wonder why you wasted your time for staying so long.

I was always told, just because something is a "good" thing does NOT mean it is a "God" thing. Just because Z displayed some "good" characteristics does NOT mean that was the husband "God" wanted me to be with for the remainder of my life. God really is a Protector when you diligently seek Him and seek Him first.

Warning always comes before destruction. Pay attention to the warnings and patterns so you will not be destroyed spiritually, mentally, physically, or emotionally.

There's a HUGE difference between a person that is domineering and a person of strength. Strong men and women aren't always appreciated. A REAL person will appreciate your strength. Do not ever minimize yourself for the approval of someone else. The things that are beneficial to the relationship are your courage, honesty, and love. You do not need to focus on the person that allowed you to walk out of their life because they could not handle your strength. That is their loss for not recognizing you are truly amazing! Surround yourself by an individual that will empower you, help you see the best in yourself, and cherish you. You are always there for other people so now let someone be there for you. I want you to know there is a special person that will appreciate you. They will appreciate you not only by what comes out of their mouth but also by what they do.

Get far away from people that take advantage of your value!

BOOKING INFORMATION

For Empowerment Speaking Engagements

Contact Me:

devchestnut@gmail.com

or

(786) 507 – 8204

devonchestnut.com

Follow me on:

FB: @ladies4apurpose

IG: Devon__Chestnut

Twitter: Devon__Chestnut

ACKNOWLEDGMENTS

Boaz Brand – photo shoot and book cover.

Elevate Marketing -

https://squareup.com/store/elevatemarketing

Will Ellis Jr. –back cover model. wmeellisjr@gmail.com

79088065R00057

Made in the USA
Lexington, KY
17 January 2018